A YEAR IN THE LIFE OF Worcestershire's Nature Reserves

Written and edited by **G.H. Green**

Photographs by **David M. Green**

Line drawings by **R.M. Bishop** and **Brett Westwood**

Worcestershire Wildlife Trust

PISCES PUBLICATIONS

Pisces Publications is the imprint of the Nature Conservation Bureau Limited

First published by Pisces Publications 1995 for Worcestershire Wildlife Trust.
Pisces Publications is the imprint of the Nature Conservation Bureau Limited.

British Library-in-Publication Data.
A catalogue record for this book is available from the British Library.

ISBN 1 874357 08 0

Designed and produced by the Nature Conservation Bureau Limited,
36 Kingfisher Court, Hambridge Road, Newbury, Berkshire, RG14 5SJ.

Printed in Hong Kong for Alan Sutton Publishing Ltd.

Cover photographs
Front: Nuthatch © Dennis Bright.
Back: Wild daffodils in spring in the Duke of York Meadow © David M. Green.

Contents

page

iv Acknowledgements
1 Introduction
3 Worcestershire and its wildlife
6 Aileshurst Coppice
10 Avoncroft Wildflower Meadow
12 Badgers Hill
14 Beaconwood and The Winsel
17 The Betts Reserve
20 Briar Hill Coppice
22 Broadmoor Wood
24 Broadway Gravel Pit
28 The Brotheridge Green Reserves
33 Chance Wood
34 Christopher Cadbury Wetland Reserve, Upton Warren
40 Cleeve Prior
42 The Devil's Spittleful and Rifle Range
48 Duke of York Meadow
49 Eades Meadow and Foster's Green Meadows
52 Feckenham Wylde Moor
56 Grovely Dingle
57 Hornhill Wood
64 Hunthouse Wood
68 Ipsley Alders Marsh
70 The Knapp and Papermill
77 Knowles Coppice
80 Lion Wood
81 The Long Meadow
84 The Marsh Warbler Reserves and Nafford Island
86 Mill Meadow
88 Monkwood
93 Newbourne Wood
94 Penny Hill Bank
96 Poolhay Meadows
97 Randan Wood
100 Ravenshill Nature Reserve
104 Spinneyfield
105 Tiddesley Wood
112 Trench Wood
116 Tunnel Hill Meadow
118 Wilden Marsh
120 Windmill Hill

Acknowledgements

The most important parts of this book are the accounts written by volunteer reserve managers or wardens listed below. I am very grateful to them all for their contributions to the book and for supporting the work of the Trust so well. Welding all these accounts into a book has been an interesting task. For reasons of cost the size of the book has had to be restricted. Many excellent accounts have therefore, regretfully, had to be edited and shortened. I hope the authors will not be too disappointed with the final result. The original texts will be placed in the Trust's library.

Many thanks to my friends, collaborators and illustrators Brett Westwood and Ray Bishop, for their ever-tolerant support and help, and to David Green for travelling the county to take photographs of the reserves.

Many thanks to Colin Raven, Director of the Worcestershire Wildlife Trust, for his friendly support, assistance, encouragement and advice, and to Janice King for converting some very remarkable scripts into something legible! Also Helen Woodman, the Trust's Reserves Officer, for her support.

Thanks also to our publishers, the Nature Conservation Bureau Limited, especially Peter Creed, for believing in the project. Peter and also Martin Harvey gave excellent support in designing and preparing the book.

G.H. GREEN April 1995

Contributors

Reserve diaries:
Peter Auger (Eades Meadow and Foster's Green Meadows), Keith Barnett (Aileshurst Coppice), Mike Bretherton (Feckenham Wylde Moor), Bill Brown (Beaconwood and The Winsel; Spinneyfield), Tessa Carrick (Avoncroft Wildflower Meadow), Sue Clark (Ravenshill Nature Reserve), Stuart Corbett (Mill Meadow), Arthur Cundall (Tunnel Hill Meadow), Nigel Davies and Roger Robinson (Wilden Marsh), Fred Fincher (Randan Wood), Eric Hawkeswood (Grovely Dingle), Tom Haynes (Hornhill Wood), John Hodson (The Marsh Warbler Reserves), Elisabeth Jackson (The Long Meadow), Tony Jackson (Ipsley Alders Marsh; Lion Wood), Terry Jennings and Betty Ballard (Badgers Hill), Terry Knight (Windmill Hill), Rosalind Knowlson (Brotheridge Green Old Railway), Linda Lewis (Melrose Farm Meadows), Helen Mackeness (The Betts Reserve), Colin and Heather Raven (The Knapp and Papermill), Bert Reid (Tiddesley Wood), Roger Robinson, Chris Bradley and Sylvia Sheldon (Knowles Coppice), Andrew Santer (Hunthouse Wood), Dave Scott (The Devil's Spittleful and Rifle Range), Jane and Dave Scott (Penny Hill Bank), Alan Shepherd (Christopher Cadbury Wetland Reserve, Upton Warren), Dorothy Snaddon (Newbourne Wood), Ken Thomas (Trench Wood), Geoff Trevis (Briar Hill Coppice), Claire Turner and Mike Williams (Monkwood), Mark Turner (Broadway Gravel Pit) and Bob Woodroofe (Cleeve Prior).

Photographs:
Duke of York Meadow (page 3), common spotted-orchid (page 3), yellow star-of-Bethlehem (page 6), knapweed (page 11), Beaconwood (page 14), The Betts Reserve (page 18), Broadway Gravel Pit (page 27), Brotheridge Green Old Railway (page 30), Boynes Meadow (page 31), Christopher Cadbury Wetland Reserve, Upton Warren (pages 34, 39), Devil's Spittleful and Rifle Range (pages 42, 46), Eades Meadow (page 50), green-winged orchids (page 51), Feckenham Wylde Moor (page 54), Hornhill Wood (page 58), Hunthouse Wood (page 66), The Knapp (page 74), Knowles Coppice (page 79), The Long Meadow (page 82), Mill Meadow (page 87), Monkwood (page 90), Penny Hill Bank (page 95), bluebell (page 98), Randan Wood (page 99), Tiddesley Wood (pages 106, 111), orange-tip (page 107), Trench Wood (page 114), brown birch bolete (page 115), Wilden Marsh (page 119), Windmill Hill (page 122) © David M. Green. Purple hairstreak (page 59), pearl-bordered fritillary (page 67), white admiral (page 110) © Jim Asher. Great spotted woodpecker (page 103) © BBONT. Dipper (page 19), emperor dragonfly (page 55), nuthatch (page 62), kingfisher (page 70) © Dennis Bright. Wood anemone (page 23), oak eggar (page 47), fallow deer (page 78), wood whites (page 91), herb-Paris (page 102), woolly thistle (page 123) © Peter Creed. Blackthorn (page 83) © Bob Gibbons/Natural Image. Primrose (page 63) © G.H. Green. Dormouse (page 75) © Pat Morris. Redstart (page 3), shoveler (page 38) © Mike Read.

Line drawings:
Ray Bishop and Brett Westwood. Peter Creed, Charlotte Matthews and Lee Scott.

Editorial assistance:
Brett Westwood and Colin Raven. Martin Harvey and Peter Creed at the Nature Conservation Bureau Limited.

Maps prepared by the Nature Conservation Bureau Limited.

Introduction

This book is a celebration of the Worcestershire Wildlife Trust's nature reserves, compiled during the Trust's Silver Jubilee Year 1993–1994. By its 25th year the Trust has established nearly 60 reserves covering about 600 hectares (1,500 acres) of the best wildlife sites in the old county of Worcestershire.

These reserves are exceptional and beautiful places. One is a National Nature Reserve, many are designated Sites of Special Scientific Interest (SSSIs) by English Nature, the government's conservation organisation. This designation recognises their national importance for wildlife. These and the non-SSSI reserves are all Special Wildlife Sites recognised by the Trust and Local Government as important places in the county.

Whenever possible the Trust wants people to visit its reserves to enjoy their wildlife and the peace and quiet of the countryside. Many of the reserves are open to both members of the Trust and the public but some have restricted access, usually because open access would damage the wildlife the Trust strives to conserve, or the Trust is bound by special covenants, or there are access difficulties. The Trust does not willingly restrict access so it is essential that potential visitors pay heed to the few restrictions placed on them. It is often possible to obtain a special permit from the Trust's office to visit those reserves with restricted access.

To maintain legal control over rights of way and access all the Trust's reserves are closed to the public on Christmas Day.

The reserves

The major part of this book is made up of illustrated accounts from each reserve, and the bulk of each account is usually a diary written by a volunteer reserve manager or warden. Each diary is highly individual and reflects the interests and enthusiasms of the writer. Some describe visits on particular days through the year, some give monthly accounts, others give seasonal descriptions. In some cases a general account written by the editor is all that is available. The accounts vary a great deal in length. All are fascinating as they reflect the views of people very familiar with "their" reserve.

The reserves are arranged in alphabetical order. Each account starts with a short introduction, and information on access. This book is not intended to be a detailed guide to the reserves, or a reserves handbook. We hope it is an attractive and interesting account of the reserves in Silver Jubilee Year April 1993 to March 1994. We defy any reader, however well they know Worcestershire, not to learn something new about its diverse natural history from this book.

Visiting the reserves

Please keep to paths and follow the Countryside Code. Where there is restricted access please adhere to permit arrangements as they are designed for the protection of wildlife not to keep you out! If you want to make a special visit please contact the Trust's Reserve Officer. If you write to the Trust please send a stamped and addressed envelope.

If you take a dog to a reserve please keep it under control. Uncontrolled dogs disturb wildlife and may harass other visitors. Please do not use wildlife reserves simply as dog latrines as this can be very unpleasant for other visitors. Ideally dogs should be kept on leads but we realise this may not be practical.

Visitors should normally proceed on foot. Horses are not allowed on reserves (except on public bridleways) and neither are mountain bikes or any other vehicles, except during special activities. These restrictions are not made to annoy visitors but to prevent undue damage and disturbance to the reserve and its wildlife. Car parks are provided at a few reserves. Several reserves are accessible to people in wheelchairs.

Health and safety

For your own safety you are advised to take care when visiting reserves. The paths and tracks may be muddy and slippery and you should wear stout suitable footwear. Do not leave the paths and tracks and please adhere to any signs and instructions.

The woodlands are often used for a mixture of wildlife conservation, forestry and for visitors. It is essential that you do not approach people engaged in forestry activities such as tree-felling. If they are using chain-saws, tractors or other machinery they may not hear you approach and you could be in serious risk of injury. Do not allow children to climb onto piles of timber along the rides as these may be unstable and fall.

If you go alone to a reserve, especially the larger, wilder and more remote sites, you are advised to inform somebody where you are going so that you can be found more easily if you fall or are taken ill.

Follow the Country Code

Guard against all risk of fire.

Fasten all gates.

Keep your dogs under close control.

Keep to public footpaths.

Use gates and stiles to cross fences, hedges, and walls.

Leave livestock, crops and machinery alone.

Take your litter home.

Help to keep all water clean.

Protect wildlife, plants and trees.

Take special care on country roads.

Make no unnecessary noise.

We are sure all visitors will appreciate that flowers should not be picked.

Information

The Trust is always interested to hear of any observations you may make on reserves. Please write to us at the Trust's office, preferably enclosing a stamped and addressed envelope if you would like a reply. If you observe any untoward activities on a reserve please let us know or report it to the police. Be aware of the illegal activities of badger diggers and if you see such activity do not tackle the people yourself but let the police and the Trust know as quickly as possible.

Hunting and shooting are not usually permitted on the Trust's reserves. Occasionally, because of special arrangement with owners, we are not in a position to prevent such activities.

The Worcestershire Wildlife Trust

The Worcestershire Wildlife Trust is the marketing name for the Worcestershire Nature Conservation Trust Ltd., founded in 1968 and registered in England as a charity and company limited by guarantee. Charity number 256618, company number 929644.

The aims of the Trust are:

- ◆ To maintain natural places in Worcestershire by establishing wildlife reserves and encouraging others to do so.
- ◆ To ensure that land owners, users and planners are aware of the need for wildlife conservation.
- ◆ To help everyone to understand and appreciate the need for wildlife conservation, and to encourage them to either take part in the Trust's work or to support its activities.
- ◆ To carry out natural history surveys so as to be fully aware of the county's wildlife resources, and to have the data on which to base advice to land users and for the selection of nature reserves.
- ◆ To attain these ends the Trust needs wide support and many members. Over 5,000 people are now subscribing members of the Trust. Far more are needed if the Trust's work and influence on wildlife conservation in Worcestershire is to continue to grow and thrive.

If you would like more information about the Trust please write to Worcestershire Wildlife Trust, Lower Smite Farm, Smite Hill, Hindlip, Worcester, WR3 8SZ.

The Trust is a corporate member of The Wildlife Trusts, the largest voluntary organisation in the UK concerned with all aspects of wildlife protection.

Worcestershire and its wildlife

The old county of Worcestershire will soon reappear in its own right following its shot-gun marriage with Herefordshire in 1974 and its impending divorce following the 1995 report by the local government review. The main body of the county is roughly rectangular: about 32 miles north to south and 23 miles east to west, with a 12-mile long horn projecting westwards along the Teme valley to Tenbury Wells.

The bulk of Worcestershire is a low-lying saucer of land drained by the Rivers Severn, Avon and Teme. It is encircled by low hills reaching 300 metres above sea level in a few places and open to the south, where the River Severn flows into the Plain of Gloucester. To the west the county is hilly with deep-cut valleys. Within a relatively small area Worcestershire is very varied in geology, soil types and appearance. The central plain is mainly of heavy Keuper Marls and Liassic Clays with an intermittent cover of 'drift' material derived from the glaciers and rivers of the past. In the Kidderminster area the soils are more sandy and free-draining and once supported extensive areas of heathland.

To the west ancient hard rocks form the familiar skyline of the Malvern Hills, and hilly countryside extends north to the coal-bearing rocks of the Wyre Forest in the north-west, and to the northern Clent and Lickey Hills. In the east the limestone Cotswold escarpment is a prominent feature, mainly just beyond the county boundary but enclosed within the county at Broadway with structurally similar outliers such as Bredon Hill.

The present-day geomorphology of the county is a legacy of the last ice age which retreated about 10,000 years ago. Following the retreat of the ice the county gradually became heavily wooded with extensive wetlands on the lower-lying ground. Since about 5,000 years ago man has drained the county, felled most of the woodland and converted the original wild landscape to an agricultural one. A pattern of cultivation and woodland gradually emerged and eventually formed the characteristic English landscape by perhaps 1,000 years ago. This became fossilised by the enclosure acts of about

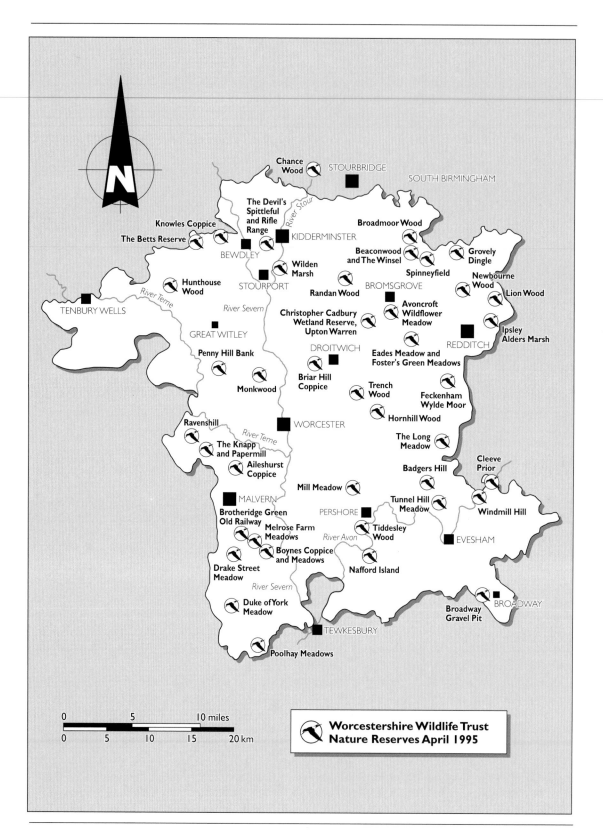

Chance
Wood
STOURBRIDGE
SOUTH BIRMINGHAM

The Devil's
Spittleful
and Rifle
Range
Broadmoor Wood

Knowles Coppice
KIDDERMINSTER
Beaconwood
and The Winsel
Grovely
Dingle

The Betts Reserve
Spinneyfield
Newbourne
Wood

BEWDLEY
Wilden
Marsh
BROMSGROVE
Lion Wood

Hunthouse
Wood
STOURPORT
Randan Wood
Avoncroft
Wildflower
Meadow

TENBURY WELLS
River Teme
River Severn
Christopher Cadbury
Wetland Reserve,
Upton Warren
Ipsley
Alders Marsh

GREAT WITLEY
DROITWICH
Eades Meadow and
Foster's Green Meadows
REDDITCH

Penny Hill Bank
Briar Hill
Coppice
Trench
Wood
Feckenham
Wylde Moor

Monkwood
Hornhill Wood

Ravenshill
River Teme
WORCESTER
The Long
Meadow

The Knapp
and Papermill
Badgers Hill
Cleeve
Prior

Aileshurst
Coppice
Mill Meadow
Tunnel Hill
Meadow
Windmill Hill

MALVERN
PERSHORE
EVESHAM

Brotheridge Green
Old Railway
Tiddesley
Wood

Melrose Farm
Meadows
River Avon

Boynes Coppice
and Meadows
Nafford Island

Drake Street
Meadow
River Severn

Duke of York
Meadow
Broadway
Gravel Pit
BROADWAY

TEWKESBURY

Poolhay Meadows

0   5   10 miles
0   5   10   15   20 km

**Worcestershire Wildlife Trust
Nature Reserves April 1995**

150 years ago. However, in the last fifty years much of the old English landscape has been swept away by modern intensive agriculture, expanding towns and villages, and new roads. The county beloved by the Victorian naturalists for its luxuriant and abundant wildlife is now much changed and wildlife hangs on by its fingertips in the remnants of ancient woods, pastures, heaths, marshes, and in odd corners which have escaped the modern agricultural revolution.

Because of its varied geology and soils, and because of its geographical location, Worcestershire supports a very varied wildlife and is a transition zone where plants and animals of differing distributions meet. A glance at modern atlases of plant and animal distribution is revealing. Species characteristic of the highlands of Wales creep into the western fringes. Those with south-eastern distributions in England start to peter out in Worcestershire. Under the influence of the Severn Estuary the mild climate enables species with south-western distributions to extend into the heart of England.

The effects of local land structure and soils are striking. Those species (many mosses and ferns) which thrive in deep shaded damp valleys are found along the Teme Valley but not in the central plain. Those of sandy well-drained soils grow near Kidderminster but not on clays near Pershore. The grasses of the thin acid soils of the Malvern Hills are very different from those on the alkaline limy soils of Bredon Hill. Native small-leaved lime trees are common west of the Severn but rare to the east. Central Worcestershire woods are usually derelict hazel coppice with oak standards. The westerly woods are very varied with more lime, wych elm and ash mixed with oak.

Worcestershire has a special responsibility for old meadows on lowland neutral soils. These were once very abundant in central Worcestershire but now only 2–3% remain undestroyed by modern agriculture. Their rich and varied swards are rich in flowers and grasses and characterised by green-veined orchids. The prime example is the Trust's reserve now called The Fosters Green National Nature Reserve, with the great Eades hay meadow unsurpassed in the county.

Worcestershire contains large parts of three big rivers. The River Severn and River Avon are both highly managed rivers with locks and weirs, and carry heavy loads from sewage outfalls. The Severn receives the highly polluted waters of the River Stour which drains the Black Country in the West Midlands. In contrast the pure waters of the River Teme join the Severn just south of Worcester. The glorious Teme is in a more or less natural state with deeps, riffles and gravel bars. Thankfully the water quality of the Severn and Avon has improved and otters are slowly returning to the county.

Apart from the rivers Worcestershire is a fairly dry county with no large natural lakes. Compensation for this shortfall is found in canal feeder reservoirs at Bittell and Tardebigge, in ornamental pools like Westwood Great Pool, and in the subsidence pools at Upton Warren. The latter is the county's most important wetland reserve and is owned by the Trust. Marshes are now rare and the Trust is pleased to conserve those at Wilden, Upton Warren, Feckenham, and Ipsley Alders in Redditch.

There are many other examples of Worcestershire's riches and one of the natural history excitements is to discover them amongst the county's cultivated fields. The conservation challenge is to ensure that space is left for all aspects of the county's wildlife among man's activities.

The aim of present-day nature conservationists is to stem the tide which is still sweeping wildlife away, and to encourage everyone to leave space for wildlife on their land. This philosophy has gained much ground in public opinion over the last 20 years. There have been gains. In places farmers now encourage wildlife; there are many beneficial changes in woodland management; attitudes to river and watercourse management have improved dramatically; pools are being created; developers take care of important sites; local authorities include nature conservation in local land-use plans; environmental impact studies are now commonplace. In practice much remains to be done especially on most farmland, but there is hope of improvement in the future if some land is either cultivated less intensively or taken out of agriculture because of over-production and used for more wildlife-friendly purposes.

Through its work the Worcestershire Wildlife Trust encourages everyone to think about wildlife conservation and to act in its favour. Part of the Trust's work is the establishment of nature reserves. The aim is to conserve a good range of Worcestershire's habitats so ensuring their survival and, whenever possible, to open the reserves for people to visit and enjoy. The Trust is convinced that showing the wonders of wildlife to everyone will influence future land management for the better.

In such a varied county as Worcestershire it is difficult for the Trust to obtain good examples of all habitats as reserves, and also expensive far beyond the Trust's present resources.

We try to lead by example. We hope you will visit our reserves and feel moved to create your own, and to support the Trust in its work, so that the celebrations after the next 25 years will be even greater.

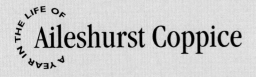

Aileshurst Coppice

This small 1½ hectare wood is about ¼ mile south-west of Leigh Sinton. It was bought by the Trust in 1973, to protect the yellow star-of-Bethlehem. Because of the presence of this rare plant the site has been designated as an SSSI. The reserve is situated on the Keuper Marl, a kind of limy clay. The woodland is of oak and ash trees with hazel and elm coppice, bordered by a meandering stream.

Because the reserve is so small, and because the ground flora will be easily damaged by trampling, access has to be restricted. All visitors must apply to the Trust's office for a permit to visit.

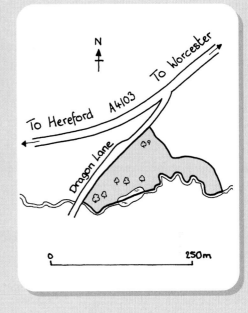

by Keith Barnett

12 March 1993

My first visit to Aileshurst Coppice was to carry out the annual count of yellow star-of-Bethlehem. This nationally uncommon plant grows in cool, damp and well-drained woods, pastures and limestone pavements. In Worcestershire it is extremely rare and now grows, so far as I know, only in Aileshurst Coppice.

I was delighted to find the first patch of about 20 plants near the metal entrance gate. Yellow star-of-Bethlehem is a small bulbous perennial plant, about 15 cm high, with umbel-like clusters of greenish-yellow star-shaped flowers.

Ramsons

The flowering period varies considerably and flowers have been known to be out at Aileshurst as late as the third week in April. This year timing was spot on and after an hour or so I had counted 75 flowering heads plus another 15 or so on private land on the other side of the stream. A count of 90 is about average: in good years there can be many more and in 1972 there were 216. The plant's requirements are pretty exacting as it needs to have its roots in shade and its head in the sun. It does not seem to set seed in this country and reproduces by means of small bulbils situated at the base of the parent plant.

Aileshurst is a very pretty wood, with masses of bluebells and ramsons Some of the bluebells were beginning to open, scenting the air with their own delicious perfume. The leathery dark-green evergreen shrub spurge-laurel, scarce in Worcestershire, was in bloom, and "smiling their lives away" at my feet were violets, primroses, delicately fragrant wood anemones and lesser celandines.

There is a wide variety of trees and shrubs: wych elm, English elm, wild service-tree, silver birch, downy birch, ash, oak, holly, grey willow, hawthorn, midland hawthorn, crab apple, blackthorn, guelder-rose, dogwood, elder, hazel and lots of spindle and field maple. I found a number of red currant bushes, almost certainly truly wild, and I shall be interested to see how much fruit is produced later on (and what it tastes like!).

19 April

The reserve looked quite magnificent and the bluebells which were only just beginning to open last month were now at their peak. It is difficult to describe a bluebell wood without lapsing into cliches, but we are indeed fortunate in this country to be able to enjoy such a sight. There were countless thousands of flowers, mostly the familiar blue but with a smattering of white, and every so often a wonderful perfume on the air. Unfortunately, quite a lot of trampling had occurred and although this is inevitable on the paths it is less easy to understand why there should have been so many flattened plants away from these.

Bluebell

As to the flora, it was pleasing to see that apart from the primroses, which looked even better than last month (including one of the unusual pink variety), many other spring flowers were coming out. The brilliant white stars of greater stitchwort caught my eye. Stitchwort used to be drunk with wine to cure the stitch. Other old Worcestershire names include bird's-eye, moon-flower, scurvy-grass and snake-flower. The butter-yellow flowers of yellow archangel were also out, and this species is a well-known indicator of ancient and undisturbed woodland. The leaves of wild angelica and meadowsweet could be seen in a damp area near to the stream. Angelica was chewed by the people of London in a vain attempt to protect them against the Great Plague of 1665. Meadowsweet is amusingly called courtship-and-matrimony in Cumberland, because although the flowers smell very sweet before they are picked, they then very quickly lose their fragrance! The red currants I saw last month are now in flower. Of the yellow star-of-Bethlehem, nothing could now be seen: all flowers had gone over and the superficial similarity of the leaves to those of bluebell make identification extremely difficult.

I saw a rabbit scurrying away into the undergrowth and heard the calls – so lacking any melody they are hardly songs – of the cuckoo, great tit and pheasant. The cuckoo is early in Worcestershire this year and I first heard one in my garden in Malvern on 3 April.

13 May

It was appreciably shadier inside the wood than last month and much more difficult to navigate through the thick vegetation, and although I managed to walk all of the paths, only the northern one (alongside Dragon Lane) was really easy. The others were waist-high in cow parsley, which is not too bad, and stinging nettles, which is a different matter! On this visit I made a point of looking for the early-purple orchid, for which there is an old record, and the wild service-tree which is a feature of the wood, a rare tree and an indicator of ancient woodland. I had no luck with the orchid, surprisingly, I think, since the site looks ideal, and it has flowered well elsewhere this year. I found the service-tree in flower, a mature specimen about 15 metres high (they can reach 25 metres or more), by the northern path. The

Spindle

wild service-tree is related to the rowan or mountain ash but with maple-like leaves and attractive white hawthorn-like flowers and inconspicuous brown spotted fruits edible when fully ripe. These fruits have an interesting history and when the tree was commoner than now they were widely sold in country markets and used to make jams and jellies. They could also be made into a cider-like drink or steeped in brandy to make a fruit liqueur. Service-tree wood is tough, yellowish-white streaked with brown, and is highly valued. In Worcestershire the tree used to be called lizzory, lessory or whitty-pear. The name *service* comes from the Anglo-Saxon word *syrfe*, derived from the Latin *sorbea*, the tree having been known medicinally to the Romans.

Plants in the shrub layer and in bud included dogwood, privet and spindle. Spindle wood is white or pale yellow, and being so hard was formerly used for spindles before the invention of the spinning-wheel, and is still used for knitting needles, pegs and manicure sticks. Its fine-grained charcoal is used by artists. In autumn it produces one of the most spectacular of our native fruits, a four-lobed pink capsule with orange-coated seeds called by the French "Priest's Hat".

Aileshurst has a rich ground flora, and noteworthy flowers seen for the first time this year were wood speedwell, cuckooflower, wood spurge (at its peak), common mouse-ear, three-nerved sandwort, and particularly pleasing, because it is a new record for the reserve, bugle (a fine spike on the northern path).

Wood avens, which is common in the wood, was just beginning to flower. The root of this plant has a strong clove carnation scent and is used in Benedictine and other alcoholic drinks. It was once called *herba benedicta*, blessed herb, being a medieval remedy for a number of ailments, and is still known as herb-bennet.

8 June

A very hot and sultry day at the beginning of a short heat wave. Conditions inside the wood were, however, much cooler in the dappled shade and it was very pleasant even though the going was a little difficult because of the strong growth of vegetation, particularly nettles and brambles.

As usual, I first of all looked at the hedge abutting Dragon Lane and found the buckthorn planted by a former warden in 1979. This seems entirely at home, as indeed it should as it is a lime-lover and Aileshurst's soil is calcareous. Buckthorn is the food plant of the caterpillar of the brimstone butterfly. Its name has nothing to do with male deer or any other animal, but is an early mistranslation of the German name for the plant *buxdorn*, thorn-bearing box-tree. The black bryony I noticed last time clambering ten feet up the bank was now almost out. Black bryony's flowers are in fact greenish-yellow, and it gets its name from the dark-coloured rootstock. The spikes of lords-and-ladies were full of green berries which will later turn orange and then a vivid scarlet. These were formerly used to make starch. Elizabeth I's

Buckthorn

familiar ruff would probably have been stiffened with this.

Inside the wood, most of the glorious spring display was over and there were no more bluebell or ramsons flowers to be seen. All that was left was a sticky mess of trampled and decaying leaves. It is easy to imagine how the sap of bluebells was once used by English archers to glue feathers on to arrows!

7 July

My visit coincided with the end of a long heat-wave, the temperature in Malvern having been in the high 70s and low 80s for over a fortnight. When I left, the temperature had dropped to about 68°F and it was quite windy.

The roadside verge abutting the reserve was already becoming quite autumnal, with hazel nuts forming and the green berries, which will turn red, of the black bryony. But plenty of summer flowers were still out – field-rose, replacing the earlier-flowering dog-rose, and bramble, and on the verge opposite ground elder or goutweed, greater celandine and meadowsweet. Ground elder is a native of eastern Europe introduced into Britain as a remedy for gout. It has another name, bishop's weed, a sly allusion to the supposed intemperance of the higher clergy whose excessive consumption of port was believed to cause gout!

The paths inside the wood have become all but impenetrable

Greater celandine

because of brambles. Even the hardiest of naturalists needs to protect himself against brambles and nettles, and to wear stout footwear. But the effort is worth-while. The various summer-flowering woodland grasses are well-represented at Aileshurst, and particularly eye-catching was the hairy brome, a graceful plant reaching 1½ metres high in shady spots. Almost as prominent was the giant fescue.

5 August

On my last visit of the year it rapidly became clear that it was going to be impossible without scythe or flame-thrower to penetrate more than a few feet along any of the paths. Such progress as I did manage gave me the chance to see that the codlins-and-cream (in the county also known as cherry pie) and rose-bay willowherb were now making a very nice show, and I also found wild angelica in flower near the brook. Of the helleborines there was no sign, but they may have been flourishing unseen in some inaccessible spot. On the verge opposite the reserve was a very large patch of hairy bindweed whose beautiful white trumpets are such a pleasure in the wild, although the plant is invasive and unwelcome to the gardener. At this time of year, in the brook opposite the entrance gate can be seen a good stand of hemp-agrimony and also water figwort, with some bristly oxtongue nearby. Hemp-agrimony, neither a hemp or an agrimony, is a relative of the garden Ageratum and is supposed if laid near bread to keep it fresh.

Avoncroft Wildflower Meadow

This reserve is an experiment in creative conservation. A field at the Avoncroft Museum of Buildings near Bromsgrove was stripped of fertile topsoil and seeded with a wild flower mix in an attempt to create a flower-rich meadow. Worcestershire was once rich in flowery meadows, but most grassland is now intensively cultivated and has lost many of the chracteristic grassland flowers. However, Worcestershire is still an important county for old-style meadows, a few of which are Trust reserves. The Trust began work on the Avoncroft Wildflower Meadow in 1990, funded and encouraged by Christopher Cadbury and the Croft Trust, but it was not opened as a reserve until after the Trust's Silver Jubilee Year.

This is a new reserve and arrangements for visiting the meadow have not yet been made. Please contact the Trust's office for further information. Meanwhile if you visit the Avoncroft Museum of Buildings you can lean on the gate near the windmill and look over the field.

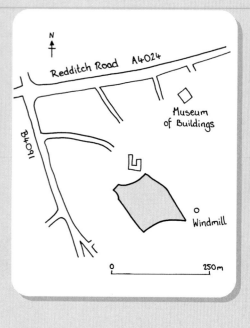

---

by Tessa Carrick

April 1994

A telephone call from John Poole, the Trust's Chief Executive: would I be prepared to look after Avoncroft Meadow if the Trust's Council decided to lease it from the Croft Trust? After initial hesitation, I agreed. Since then, it's been a year of getting to know this small patch and assessing its potential. On 9 May Council gave general approval for the leasing of Avoncroft Meadow.

Avoncroft Wildflower Meadow is new and it will be interesting to watch as the vegetation establishes itself and adjusts, maintained by the routine pattern of mowing. Perhaps, it will stimulate others to try to establish new wild flower meadows.

The field lies over Triassic Mercian Mudstones with a surface of river-washed cobbles from the River Severn Terraces. It had been sown with a rye-grass mix and treated with fertilisers as normal agricultural practice. Traditional wild flower meadows persist on fields which have not been fertilised and where the soil is fairly poor. The pattern of mowing and grazing maintains the balance and variety of grasses and flowering plants. In order to produce a wild flower meadow on this field, the top 15 cm of enriched topsoil was removed, a massive job that I would have liked to have witnessed.

The meadow is to be used in part for school visits organised by Avoncroft Museum. My first impression was not very promising,

Oxeye daisy

even in May when the grass was growing rapidly. On the face of it, eight- or nine-year olds are scarcely likely to find a meadow as exciting as a wood or a pond. It would be a challenge to get them involved.

July

The opening ceremony was performed by Chris Baines on 15 July with representatives present from the Royal Society for Nature Conservation (The Wildlife Trusts), British Coal Opencast, the Croft Trust and Avoncroft Museum, as well as a good contingent of staff and members of Worcestershire Wildlife Trust.

It was a lovely day. Though past its best, the meadow was still very attractive. There are extensive views

10

across farmland to the south and on the perimeter boundary there are a variety of statuesque trees. The windmill enhances the view. Flowers of chicory, common bird's-foot-trefoil, oxeye daisy, field scabious and greater knapweed stood out among the ten or so species of grass.

For me, nostalgia set in – the meadow reminded me of childhood dreams of being an adult, able to lie on my back in a flower-filled meadow, listening to skylarks. I suggested that a circular area should also be mown where children can sit in a group, perhaps imagining that they are field voles and thinking of their position in the food chain.

August and September

Once the knapweed had set seed, the grass was cut for hay. After the bales were collected the grass looked bleak and rather uninteresting. At the edge of the field some patches of longer grass were left to provide cover for butterflies and moths.

October and November

Ideally, a meadow should be grazed for part of the winter. Grazing creates a more uneven habitat which encourages species diversity. At Avoncroft, grazing is not permitted because of the proximity to Avoncroft Cattle Breeders stock, which must be protected from any possibility of cross-infection.

Once the meadow had been mown it became possible to inspect the field more carefully and another problem became apparent. Near the ha-ha wall forming the boundary of Avoncroft College, hay bales and debris from a previous mowing, and branches and brambles with gorse make an unsightly area which will have to be cleared.

December

This time last year I could not have imagined having a meadow to manage and watch over. Now I know more of what is involved, I'm still nervous about the prospect, but I'm looking forward to it.

So, what can I look forward to in 1995? When the grass grows up again, I hope there will be even more variety than this year. There should be plenty of people to look at it – school parties, meadow strolls conducted by volunteers, a Bromsgrove Local Group visit, a mowing event in late July, a day recording the insects and other invertebrates, a vegetation survey, and, after mowing, a grand clear-out of the area below the ha-ha wall.

Badgers Hill reserve was given to the Trust in 1978. It consists of 2.2 hectares of woodland and scrub on the edge of Bishampton Bank near Sheriff's Lench. The soils are heavy calcareous clays. The southern part of the reserve is a woodland belt, on the edge of the escarpment. At the northern end, old pasture land has been invaded by scrub. Small patches of old grassland (meadow) flora are found within the scrub and volunteers have been slowly enlarging these areas ("the Meadow") to conserve and extend the remnants of grassland flora. Ancient anthills can also be found, but few now contain ants as they were shaded-out long ago by the encroaching scrub.

Badgers Hill is situated about 2 miles south-east of Bishampton. Entry is along a rough track running due north from the road at the top of Badgers Hill, near Sheriff's Lench. Because both finding the reserve and parking are difficult visitors are advised to contact the Trust's office beforehand. The reserve is open to Trust members carrying a membership card and to those who have first obtained a permit to visit from the Trust's office.

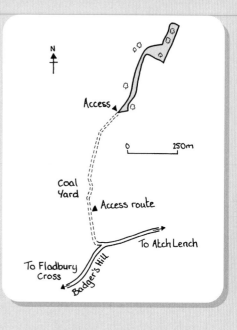

by Terry Jennings and Betty Ballard

May 1993

Met Andrew Fraser and the land agent acting for the adjacent owner to re-establish boundaries which are, as we thought, fenced to the east and south, marked by a pile of wood to the north and running along the ridge of the hill and marked by old hawthorn trees in the wood to the west.

Nest box number 235 by the meadow completely empty although there were 10 eggs on a previous visit: probably vandals as most nest material had also gone.

Lots of deer foot-prints. Andrew says large ones are probably roe deer, and the small ones muntjac which we have seen on the reserve.

Andrew confirmed identity of dyer's greenweed which is spreading in the meadow and was very pleased with the large increase in number of orchids: common spotted and twayblades.

He suggested that a future project should be to make a new meadow at top end of reserve as far away from trees as possible. Mark a grid 15×15 metres with metal pegs: list contents of each square; clear scrub and remove roots; rake away deep layer of leaves; then keep record of how plants re-colonise. As this end of the reserve still has traces of 'ridge and furrow' (therefore originally cultivated) and as the other meadow is so rich in plants we may in time see a second meadow come into being.

Peacock

June

Plants noted in full flower: dog-roses, burdock, herb-Robert, elder, hedge bedstraw, St John's-wort, oxeye daisy, agrimony, common milkwort, meadow vetchling, twayblades, honeysuckle, rowan.

Lots of chiffchaffs as well as blue tits, long-tailed tits and a jenny wren.

Seven nest boxes used out of 15 (all blue tits).

Bonfire from last November completely flat with a circle of thistles around the line of fire.

July

The ground is very hard now with lots of big cracks despite the wet season. Dave strimmed path through to the meadow but the walk through the trees is very dark indeed. The leaf canopy is very dense and casts a very gloomy feel to the first part of the wood with lots of bramble. In contrast the meadow is a glorious riot of colour in the sun with hardheads in full colour and a lot of agrimony and St John's-wort. Far side of the reserve also has a very heavy leaf cover, though with a different feel since much of it is hawthorn and elder so in the sun one gets a soft dappled feel. The wooded area to the south of the meadow has nettles growing under the trees – the leaf cover is less dense with little bramble. In fact the three areas of wood have very different 'feels' to them.

August

Still no more boundary markers – guess the land agents don't want to tackle the brambles! Badger dropping again at far end of reserve so for this reason, and because of the density of shrub cover, decided on a less dense area close to existing meadow to mark out for 'new' meadow, 15 metres square. This area has three fern plants (will probably be moved), a few small sedges, one violet plant but no other small plants. Only one turkey oak (small) would need to be removed, the rest being hawthorn scrub.

Four dragonflies seen in meadow – this is the first time we remember seeing these – perhaps the water on the nearby new golf course could be the reason. A frog was also seen – also a first for us.

Hawthorn

October

Warm sunny day following a long wet spell. Lots of deer prints along

drive to reserve plus horse prints. Rowan leaves at entrance of reserve starting to change colour. Saw four squirrels along path. Squirrel dray half way along.

Fungi found included candle snuff under trees, *Clitocybe flaccida* and *Laccaria laccata* on main path, and *Daldinia concentrica* in the area just before the meadow.

November

Ten people on work party. Cleared the meadow in record time but despite several efforts could not get fire to burn well and had to leave it smouldering in the centre – dinner potatoes uncooked!

Terry cleared trees in area adjoining meadow to make a new glade. Trunks dropped around edges to make seats and brush pulled back to leave a cleared area.

Found signs of badgers getting over the wire in north-east corner of the reserve and using the wood as a latrine.

December

Very hard frost overnight leaving all but the very wet patch on corner by land drain hard and easy to walk on. Very bright sunny day.

Lots of disturbance to leaves on footpaths by animals. Quite a lot of branches down off trees following strong winds of a week or so ago including one off tree in new glade.

Centre of fire from last work party had burnt through – potatoes eaten and deer dung left in centre.

February 1994

Hawthorn in bud along the path. Bluebells about 3 cm out of ground. Lots of muntjac deer prints on path. Orchid leaf about halfway along lower path 5 cm out.

Muntjac

In the glade lots of deer prints. Nettles and lords-and-ladies showing. Many signs of deer. In the meadow cowslips just showing.

On top path rain water has washed a lot of soil off the field onto the corner. Lots of bluebells showing. All the nest boxes full of leaves. Box 223 used by hibernating squirrel and the hole is well chewed plus dead squirrel underneath.

Wire on gate broken down and two people shooting in the wood next door. Neighbour reported that the woodland where soil had been tipped had changed hands but they didn't know who the new owner was.

April

Cowslips flowering on edge of path just inside reserve (first time in this spot). Rowans breaking into bloom. Bluebells well into flower. Wood anemone and celandine flowering in quite large patches along pathway.

The newly cleared meadow trial area is still quite barren, with small amounts of sedge coming through. Other plants visible in small quantities include lords-and-ladies, fern, thistle, nettles, bluebells, bramble, cleavers and some elder.

Muntjac and badger tracks are widespread around the reserve also copious evidence of rabbits. There are signs of badger activity at rear of reserve (bedding material drawn clear of new workings).

Beaconwood and The Winsel

These woods are on the north-west spur of the Lickey Hills, with steep slopes rising 70 metres from pools near the A38 up to Beacon Lane. Beaconwood was cleared and replanted with oak about 120 years ago. Its soil is Clent Breccia. The Winsel is a projecting spur with plantations from about 1830. The soil is Bunter Pebble. These woods are part of the National Trust's Chadwich Estate and are managed by the Wildlife Trust under various leases.

Access is restricted to Trust members carrying a membership card and to visitors who have first obtained a permit from the Trust's office. Special public guided walks are arranged in May and September. The entrance is near Lydiate Ash, about 3 miles north of Bromsgrove, at the end of the cul de sac of the Old Birmingham Road.

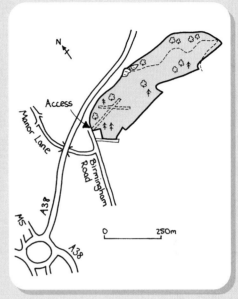

by Bill Brown

Wintertime

It's a good time to walk round when there is a light sprinkling of snow and bright winter sunshine. It is magical! You enter from the old A38 and ascend the foresters' track to the top of the Winsel, passing beech planted by E. and D. Cadbury in 1937, with a few turkey oaks and an understorey of holly. Near the top of the track the trees are more varied, with whitebeam, cherry, sweet chestnut and mature conifers on the north slope, and edged with cherry next to Beaconwood house. The south face of the Winsel was recently cleared and re-planted.

Leaving the Winsel we take the top path through the Scots pines on the ridge. With no leaves on most of the trees in winter one can see just how steep and undulating the slopes of the wood and surrounding hills are. You can see Broadmoor Wood reserve on the other side of the A38 with the Waseley Hills behind. When we reach the north boundary we return along the lower path looking across the deep dingle to Chadwich Wood where we often see a dog fox out hunting.

In the lower part of the wood are two small meadows where we are working to clear the bracken. Finally on our winter tour of the reserve we come to two pools, part of the Spring Pools on the other side of the A38. The stream is the head-water of Battlefield Brook which flows on to Bromsgrove.

Fox

Unlike most of the surrounding area the reserve is virtually undisturbed making it a haven for all wildlife, especially mammals, and it is on our walk in the snow that we can find their tracks. Resident or visiting we have fallow and muntjac deer, badger, fox, polecat, stoat, weasel and also a variety of black rabbit.

May 1993: the bluebell walk

On a Sunday in May we lead over 100 people down Beacon Lane and on to the bridle-path at Beacon Farm stopping to see our pond-dipping pool where great-crested newts are reported, and on across private land with views across to Wales.

When we enter the wood we see an unbroken sea of bluebells over 2 hectares – the perfume is overwhelming! We move on along the ridge to our great elm, a magnificent wych elm unaffected by Dutch elm disease. The oaks on the slopes have suffered from being planted on breccia and are stunted, with much deadwood, but they provide an ideal habitat for birds and insects.

Amongst the oaks are white cherries in bloom and paperbark birch with the peeling outer bark revealing the deep copper layers beneath. There are also some field maple, hawthorn and crab apple trees. Moving along the ridge past coppiced hazels (overdue for re-coppicing) and on past the Scots pines with beech and silver or downy birch, we come to our Great Oak which may be 250 years old: it was probably the marker oak at the junction of the three forestry compartments.

We carry on into the Winsel with its carpets of dead leaves where little light penetrates the conifers or dense canopy of beech leaves. Then we return to Beaconwood at it's lowest point near the pools where we might see a pair of Canada geese nesting or disturb a kingfisher on his perch. In the upper pond and along the stream we see and smell skunk cabbage, a native of North America. It has glossy bright green leaves about 75 cm high with a tall yellow spadix.

The alders round the pool are being thinned to encourage the waterside flora and pond life. We move on past the head of the side dingle where the spring rises from between the roots of a large ash. Along the path are moschatel (also called town-hall-clock), red campion, greater stitchwort and bluebells in their millions.

We then make our way uphill past the quarry and above the stream which runs all along the west edge of the reserve. On the edge of the dingle is a level area of rowan, hazel, crab apple, alder and hawthorn: a third of it is coppiced every five years to maintain an understorey to provide more cover for the wild residents.

Along the dingle spring wild flowers grow in profusion. There is wood-sorrel, wood anemone, yellow archangel and lesser celandine. Deep in the dingle there are three fine clumps of hart's-tongue fern. After we reach the north boundary, where there is a fine specimen of larch, the path turns and rises steadily up to the entrance.

Butterflies are not abundant but we have noted brimstone, purple hairstreak, holly blue, speckled wood and red admiral.

Hart's-tongue fern

Summertime
In July, August and September the reserve is left undisturbed (except for patrols by the wardens) to allow the wildlife to breed and bring up their young in peace. With the heavy leaf canopy and dense bracken on the bluebell beds it provides ideal cover for mammals and birds.

A nest-box scheme is being implemented and pied flycatchers are already in residence. A pair of buzzards were resident for five months in 1994. We have kestrel, sparrowhawk, tawny owl and little owl. Great spotted woodpeckers are present. Smaller birds include spotted flycatchers, nuthatch, treecreeper and most of the other woodland species.

Pied flycatcher

October work party
About fifteen volunteers meet at the entrance to the Winsel and are allocated their tasks by the work-party leader with a few words of advice by the safety officer. Collecting their tools they disperse to their work.

One lady is working along 200 metres of the top path with mattock and rake in preparation for the autumn guided walk. Others are cutting a new path through the holly to a side entrance. On the banks of the pool one of our qualified chainsaw operators, assisted by his safety man, is cutting down some of the big alders to let more light in. Further up the reserve another group are coppicing some hazel for demonstrations during the walk.

Before we leave we visit the reserve's most unusual resident, a giant slime mould living on a huge dead elm log. It is a creature neither animal or vegetable forming a translucent sticky mass all along the log. When it has exhausted all the nutrients in its present home it will break up and move out to find a new host.

Finally we check in our tools and make our way home, leaving the reserve in peace until next April.

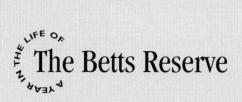

The Betts Reserve

The Betts Reserve, a 2.3 hectare wood, was purchased by the Trust in 1983 and named in memory of the late John Betts, a founder member of the Trust. The wood is a tiny but discrete part of the Wyre Forest, an extensive and important wildlife area on the Worcestershire/Shropshire border. Much of the Wyre Forest is a National Nature Reserve and SSSI. The Betts Reserve is a sessile oak woodland with some areas of hazel coppice, alder and ash. It lies on the Upper Coal Measures on a west-facing steep slope running down to alluvial areas by the Lem Brook, a tributary of Dowles Brook which it joins a little further down the valley.

The reserve is situated between the east bank of the Lem Brook, near its confluence with the Dowles Brook at Furnace Mill, and the minor road leading from Far Forest to Kinlet. Access is through a gate just north of Quarry Cottages at grid reference SO 722764. Limited car parking space by the roadside: take care. The reserve is open to visitors at all times. Please keep to the paths and take care on the steep slopes.

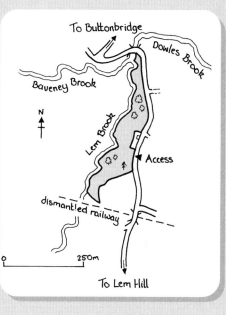

Excerpts from Helen Mackeness' notebook for 1993

January 1993

Dealing with fallen and gale-blown trees – oak, ash, alder and cherry across the Lem brook, tracks and road. Brook running very fast, high and clear yet nearby Baveney Brook very muddy. Dipper flew downstream. Flock of 50 or more excited tits, mostly blue tits, in hawthorn. Nuthatch very vocal. Saw my first bullfinch on the reserve bringing the total on bird species list to 53. Collected boxes needing repair. Planted oak saplings from my tree nursery – hard going with a layer of stone only 5 cm below the surface.

Water vole

February

Fixed metal plates round box holes in attempt to at least bruise the beaks of woodpeckers who can only engage in this vandalism for devilment. How *can* I have such affection for woodpeckers?

Three deer seen down bank and across brook – a rare and pretty sight, if only they would acquire an appetite for bramble all would be forgiven. Water vole in bank.

Snowdrops coming into bloom. Local work party continuing post and log steps on steep slopes – 120 to date on six flights. Also clearing blockage in brook caused by debris and fallen trees. What do they find to do on flat and dry reserves?

March

Daffodil month – Betts Reserve never more attractive but with so much erosion of stream banks from fallen trees and uprooted stumps many bulbs must be swept downstream after heavy rain. Somewhere else's gain perhaps. Must keep careful watch on solitary patch of toothwort perilously near edge. Find dead fox near railway embankment. Spend worried night; decide to inform police. Am 'picked up' by PC Peberdy who told me of several instances of poisoning in Wyre. Hope no one or thing has removed it, or I could be accused of 'wasting police time'. Fortunately the body still there. PC thinks it was shot and died slowly. Anemones, primroses and violets coming into bloom and the ubiquitous ramsons. Pair of grey wagtails on fallen tree, pair of

mallard on water, heron flew upstream and landed on ridiculously flimsy twig on tall oak above. 'The Woodlands' dipper flew upstream and later down and under Dowles bridge. A few nest boxes beginning to be occupied.

April

Nesting season begins in earnest. Start detailed notes for the British Trust for Ornithology nest records scheme. Brimstone and small tortoiseshell butterflies seen flying in sunshine.

Slow-worm in rubble. Green woodpecker calling; lesser spotted woodpecker chiselling at holes in dead oak. Tawny owl and young calling from near farm, goldcrest flown over Quarry Cottage. The call of the goldcrest is a rare sound since the larches were felled. Duck mallard

and seven ducklings in brook. By mid-month 14 of approximately 34 nest boxes occupied (compared with 23 in 1990). Treecreeper box specially made and donated by the late Alex Millward occupied by this species for the first time in eight years. Nest of wood chips and dry grass.

May

Garden warbler and blackcap in full song but hardly any sign of wood warbler, which up until three years ago provided dominant call throughout summer. Pair of dippers feeding, stock doves using upper owl chimney, three tawny owl chicks in lower box ringed by Jack Mountford.

Sparrowhawk dived into bramble. Squirrel raced down tree into woodpecker hole. By end of month two families had fledged –

one box of great tits and one of treecreepers. Butterflies seen include many brimstones, holly blues, speckled woods and orange-tips.

June

On 5 June show John Milner which pied flycatcher broods are ready for ringing. 12 young and one adult female ringed. What were little more than maggots a week ago will within five weeks have flown off on their own to tropical Africa! Wonder why they never line their nests with moss. On 24 June Jack does some more ringing: pied flycatchers and stock dove pair in owl box. Spotted flycatcher on wire over road – much less common than its pied cousins.

There is plenty of regrowth from coppiced oak stumps, but will they make it to provide the much needed

young specimen trees? Glorious colour from explosion of foxgloves – visited by red admiral. 15–20 metallic green banded demoiselle damselflies over water.

July

Still two late nest boxes of pied flycatchers to check. Butterflies seen include silver-washed fritillaries, gatekeepers and ringlets. Welsh gorse making spectacular increase after 1990 felling. Figwort in flower. On 11 July the last box of pied flycatchers fledged – feel lonely and desolate, must try to transfer my affections to butterflies.

August and September

The pair of stock doves which have nested in the owl box produce another brood. Endless bramble bashing.

October

Flooding after excessive rain, high water mark is 1.5 metres above the normal level. Remove mass of litter carried downstream from upstream litter louts. Few beeches survived the felling but the ones that did are glowing gloriously gold in autumn sun.

National Dormouse Week: on 31 October inspected all boxes for signs of hibernation, but no luck. Three years ago, yes. Trail of horse-chestnut seed cases along tracks, no conker trees around. I dispatched the last seedling 10 years ago, so whodunnit – squirrels or small boys?

November

Cleaning out boxes, am very popular with resident fleas. Two or three wood mouse nests.

December

Gale force winds on 9 December, several mature trees down causing obstruction.

Ringing recovery news from Jack on 22 December:

1. Female pied flycatcher which was ringed on 7 June 1989, recovered by Wychavon ringing group at Midsummer Hill (near Malvern) on 13 May 1993 at nest box on eggs.

2. Female pied flycatcher which was ringed on 6 June 1990, recovered by Wychavon Ringing Group at Midsummer Hill on 13 May 1993, for third time. Previous recoveries were on 3 June 1991 and 20 May 1992.

Here is scope for an enterprising mind to invent an avian milometer. How far had this bird flown on its migrations?

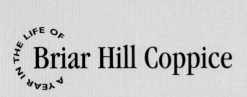

Briar Hill Coppice

Briar Hill Coppice lies to the west of Droitwich, bounded by the Droitwich by-pass (Roman Way), the River Salwarpe and the Elmbridge Brook. It is bisected by Ombersley Way from Droitwich. Grid reference SO 880624.

Cars may be parked in a small car park on the north side of Ombersley Way about half-way between the river and the canal. To get into the reserve, walk up Ombersley Way and across the river; paths lead down to the reserve on both sides of Ombersley Way. The Salwarpe Valley Nature Trail also starts from the car park and a simple trail guide, prepared jointly by the Trust and Wychavon District Council, is available from the Trust's office on receipt of a stamped and addressed envelope.

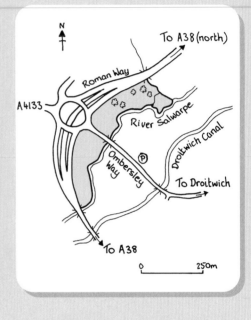

by Geoff Trevis

This reserve is a sad reminder of 'what has been lost'.

Briar Hill Coppice's main claim to fame is its location in the Salwarpe Valley. Much of this part of England overlies salt-bearing rock strata laid down in shallow seas about 200 million years ago. It is only in the Stoke Prior/Droitwich area that these strata are close enough to the surface for economic salt extraction to be possible and for saline springs to occur. This has been known and exploited since Roman times. From the wildlife point of view the most important features are the rare inland saltmarshes which developed as a result of saline water in the Salwarpe, the Droitwich Canal and the local springs, streams and ditches. Several of the plants which

have been recorded are salt-tolerant species (halophytes) normally found only at the coast. These include wild celery, Babington's orache, sea-milkwort, saltmarsh rush, dittander, reflexed saltmarsh-grass, common saltmarsh-grass, sea club-rush, Townsend's cord-grass and lesser sea-spurrey.

In recent times reflexed saltmarsh-grass and lesser sea-spurrey have been found on nearby road verges along the Droitwich by-pass, growing in areas affected by salt used to de-ice roads.

The Salwarpe Valley was first noted by Government as a site of conservation importance in its "Nature Reserves Investigation

Wild celery

Report" in 1947 and in 1954 it was recommended as an SSSI by Mr Fred Fincher and others. An area of about 30 hectares, stretching from Salwarpe Church to Briar Mill, was scheduled in 1956. Between then and 1970, despite proposals for its designation as a Local Nature Reserve, damaging operations were carried out including drainage and spraying with insecticides. In 1972 the area of SSSI was reduced to 19 hectares. Road building, drainage and levelling for playing fields continued until in 1980 the area of land assessed as being of scientific value was below 4 hectares (mainly in and around Briar Hill Coppice). It was finally de-scheduled in 1986.

Nonetheless, much of the site has continued to be of wildlife importance; for example, the reedbeds along the Salwarpe Canal supported one of the largest reed warbler colonies in the county, now reduced due to canal improvement works. The importance of the area was recognised in 1973 when Briar Hill Coppice nature reserve was established by agreement between the local council and the Worcestershire Nature Conservation Trust. The majority of the saltmarsh plants had been lost but one of the most notable, dittander, is still common and wild celery can be found at the water's edge in some years. There may be others lurking in odd corners waiting to be rediscovered.

Attitudes to conservation among planners and the public changed considerably during the 1970s and 1980s. Discussions between the Trust, the local council and the Droitwich Canal Trust were started and the unique opportunity which this offered to develop a wildlife reserve for the enjoyment of local people was recognised. In 1984 a nature trail was opened which was designed by the Trust and funded by Wychavon District Council. Although now somewhat difficult to follow, the trail is still there and the whole area remains open to the public, including Briar Hill Coppice reserve.

Despite the damage done over 40 years the Salwarpe Valley in this area is a place of exceptional interest with grassland, scrub, woodland, canal and river. Briar Hill Coppice probably preserves the most interesting remnant of the old SSSI.

With continuing cooperation between the Trust and the Local Authority this unique site with its remaining saltmarsh plants will continue undeveloped and available for the enjoyment of all.

The reserve contains examples of several types of habitat within a very small area. The last remnant of the wood which gave its name to the site, Briar Hill Coppice, lies to the north of Ombersley Way on the steep slope from the river up to Roman Way. The wood contains some large mature poplars which show severe die-back in the crowns, probably due to the unsatisfactory nature of saline soils. The remains of old woodland flora can be seen in places, with lesser celandines, dog's mercury and giant bellflower.

Steep banks continue round Roman Way and the embankments of Ombersley Way providing patches of warm dry grassland among the trees. These areas are good for butterflies such as meadow browns and common blues, and grasshoppers can be found. The remainder of the site is wetter grassland with rushes and sedges, leading down to the river. Dittander, a tall showy plant with small cream-coloured flowers, grows on the river bank. It is a scarce plant found in Britain mainly on parts of the East Anglian coast in brackish habitats.

Unfortunately, a large number of trees have been planted many of

Dittander

which are non-native species. However, the mosaic of habitats results in an area of considerable local importance for wildlife. Many resident and migratory birds are regularly recorded and there is a rich invertebrate fauna. Water voles were commonly seen until the late 1980s but now seem to be extinct.

The Salwarpe valley nature trail starts from the car park and leads through a variety of habitats in addition to Briar Hill Coppice. Part of the trail follows the canal. There are common reeds and other water plants along the margins. The slow-moving water creates pond-like conditions and freshwater invertebrates such as dragonfly nymphs and water scorpions can be found. Reed and sedge warblers nest in the small reedbeds. Further on, the trail dips down to the faster-flowing river Salwarpe. Damp ground nearby is covered with tall rank vegetation in summer, with burdock and hemlock. Also near the river are patches of butterburs which push up spikes of pinkish flowers in spring followed by huge rhubarb-like leaves in summer. Large hairy drinker moth caterpillars can be found in the grass and in May banded demoiselle damselflies fly by the river. Briar Hill Coppice is a small remnant of woodland with a sparse ground flora. In spring the small and curiously named plant town-hall-clock (or moschatel) grows beside the path.

A leaflet prepared jointly by the Trust and Wychavon District Council containing a map and guide is available from the Trust's office.

Sedge warbler

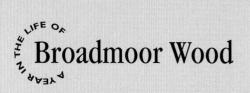
Broadmoor Wood

This 2½ hectare reserve is part of the Chadwich Estate, a National Trust property on the south-west edge of Birmingham, and is leased to the Wildlife Trust. It lies on the scarp of the south-facing Birmingham plateau in a gap, of historical importance in communications, between the Waseley Hills and Lickey Hills. Most of the wood lies on Keele clay with sandy patches, while breccia forms the west bank of the pond. Broadmoor Wood is used for wildlife studies by local schools. It is also popular with local artists in bluebell time. It is best visited in June or July when the muddy paths have dried out.

The reserve lies about a mile from the Lydiate Ash M5 motorway (junction 4). From this junction follow the A38 towards Birmingham to the top of the hill and then follow the brown County Council signs to Waseley Hill Country Park car park. Cross the St Oswald's Camp playing field opposite at grid reference SO 977766. Open to Trust members carrying membership cards. Non-members should obtain a permit from the Trust's office.

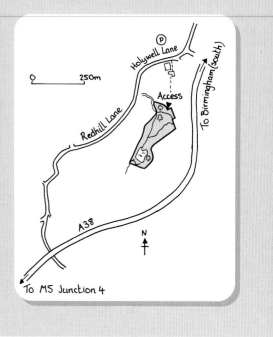

Walk through the Rubery Leisure Centre in Holywell Lane to the far side of the football pitch. Behind the goal posts note a fine belt of ash, whitebeam, field maple, cherry and oak. Between the pitch and the reserve is a small wetland area managed for invertebrates by the Trust. On a hot sunny July day it is possible to see up to eight different butterflies and also burnet and other day-flying moths, grasshoppers and damselflies. The flora includes several of the vetches, marsh and spear thistles, rush, mosses and horsetail.

On entering the wood, on your left there is an unmanaged area for comparison with the remainder of the north end of the wood, which is managed as coppice with standards. Coppicing of the hazel is done every two years on a 10-year cycle to demonstrate how the ground flora changes as the sunlight is reduced by the new growth on the coppiced stools. The standards include some fine oaks with ash, birch, rowan and hawthorn. Flowers include wood-sorrel, wood anemone, bluebells and yellow archangel, with tufted hair-grass along the paths. These are typical of woodland on a heavy clay soil.

Marsh-marigold

Leaving the higher ground we descend a flight of steps to cross a small marshy dingle, with a carpet of opposite-leaved golden-saxifrage, and pass along a narrow path cut into silty breccia which skirts the alder bog. This is a silted-up part of the uppermost of the spring pools which once provided water power for the sword mills downstream. There is a magnificent display of marsh-marigolds in the early spring.

The pool is beautiful with beds of reedmace, water horsetail, watercress and other water plants. There is a rich waterside flora along the dam.

Birds include kestrel, sparrowhawk, kingfisher, treecreeper, nuthatch, long-tailed tit, great spotted woodpecker, moorhen, coot and mallard.

Broadway Gravel Pit

Milestone Ground gravel pit at Broadway is leased by Wychavon District Council to the Trust for management as a nature reserve. It lies by the Broadway to Childswickham road in a level field. Broadway Gravel Pit was once worked to extract gravel from deposits derived from the nearby Cotswold ridge and deposited 10,000–60,000 years ago during the last Ice Ages. Although only 1.6 hectares in extent it is a wetland in a dry part of the county, and so provides living conditions for species which would otherwise not occur in the area, and a surprisingly large number of animals and plants have been found.

Broadway Gravel Pit lies on Milestone Ground, about 800 m north-west of Broadway village and on the north side of the Broadway to Childswickham road, and east of the old railway line. Access is at grid reference SP 087379 where a small fenced-off area provides parking space for 2–3 cars. Please keep to the paths. Dogs and children must be kept under control. The pools are deep and can be hazardous: take care.

by Mark Turner

March 1993

A casual visit by Christine and I on the 7th showed no surprises, but 12 species of birds and fresh frog-spawn. The water level has dropped, west side grassland being the most obvious to the eye.

During the afternoon of Saturday 13th a pair of coots were busy nest-building, presumably the female staying put on the new platform while the male brought vegetation. A treecreeper was active to the right of the hide.

We had a particularly good morning in the reserve on the rainy 21st. Although mainly a work session felling and logging three willow trees from the east side marsh, some interesting observations were made: a sparrowhawk, two jays in

west side Lombardy poplars and the reserve's first positive record of a siskin, a male, also in the top of one of the Lombardies. With muddied faces and clothes we carried the sawn-up willows through the rain from the edge of the bulrush beds to rough ground next to the hide. In all, 17 bird species were seen which I thought pretty good for a quiet part of the season.

April

At 3.15 p.m. on Thursday 8th on a mild but drizzly and overcast day we logged 16 bird species including our carrion crow on the traditional nest site in a willow top.

On the 13th birds of note were the year's first willow warbler singing

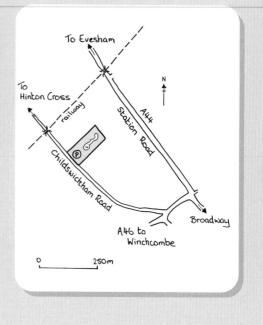

Lords-and-ladies

near the car park and two treecreepers at the reserve centre.

Our visit of 27th proved to be particularly good. Of four visible coot nests at least two, possibly three, were occupied and we now know for certain that we have five coots in the reserve. A pair of blackcaps entertained us in north end corner and four feral mallards were tame to the point of approachability. We found 16 bird species. A casual survey of plants revealed three clumps of bluebells, ground ivy, campion, white dead-nettle, plantain, flowering laburnum, lords-and-ladies growing by the car park entrance, cuckooflower along the centre trail, and three rowan saplings doing nicely along the east side trail.

May

Visit on 8th. The afternoon was mild and windy. We counted five coot's nests and were delighted to discover two adults with at least four chicks in pool 3. A pair of moorhens had a nest with at least nine eggs in the bulrushes on east side. Four drake feral mallards were present, but the biggest surprise were three adult Canada geese descending into the reserve from over the Childswickham Road. Blackcap, chiffchaff and willow warbler were all present, the latter hovering and grub collecting among willow branches around pool 1.

Moorhen

On the 11th our observations included two white butterflies, one peacock butterfly, one rabbit, one goldfinch, blue tits busy at next box number one and, to Christine's horror, a young grass snake on the path alongside pool 1.

Saturday 29th and Sunday 30th were open days at our reserve, offering guided walks to the public to help celebrate the Trust's twenty-fifth anniversary. During the hot and sunny Saturday we set up a table in the car park offering reserve guides for sale plus log books and other information for visitors to read. We had a record breaking 28 bird species on site. Highlights were a cuckoo calling and flying about the reserve when we arrived at 10 a.m., four sightings of a whitethroat, a garden warbler and a treecreeper amongst a myriad of other birds.

June

Brief visit at 8.15 a.m. on 4th, logging 12 bird species including a male whitethroat still active around nettle beds on waste ground near the car park.

The evening of the 24th was warm and sunny with no wind and swarms of flies pestered us. Fifteen bird species included whitethroat near the car park, goldfinches on thistles and five baby coots from two broods. Creeping-Jenny made a brilliant yellow carpet. Rosebay willowherb now coming into flower. We also found feverfew, white and red campion around the car park, yellow creeping cinquefoil in the car park as well as white clover and meadow crane's-bill along the trail.

July

Seventeen bird species on the 3rd but generally quiet. Highlights included a treecreeper in a willow, and a singing blackcap in willows around the edge of a pool, now a mass of blue water-speedwell.

Looking across the willow scrub from the steps we were amused to see four juvenile chiffchaffs and a juvenile blue tit, all sunning themselves on the ground with wings spread and body feathers fluffed out. Butterflies of note were marbled white, speckled wood, ringlet and small heath.

On 22nd we saw 15 bird species included a mixed tit and warbler flock, six coots, blackcap, two immature and male and female mallards and a vocal green woodpecker. Christine identified hop trefoil along the trail. We cut down grass, nettles and thistles along the footpath and sawed down some willows near the footbridges.

Blackcap

August

The water level had dropped considerably by the 8th. Of 14 bird species present, mostly young birds, blackcaps were well represented and a garden warbler seen well.

On Sunday 15th 16 bird species seen, notably a female or juvenile whitethroat hedge-skulking and calling near the entrance. A treecreeper (very vocal today), and a great spotted woodpecker flew over. On the water were four or five coots, two adult and two juvenile moorhens. A bullfinch family was quite active.

A grey heron on pool 1 took refuge in the willows before leaving. Scrub warblers were tac-tacking in the depths of vegetation and leaf warblers were calling all around. With the water getting low there are many exposed muddy areas.

September

Christopher Cole was first on site on Sunday 5th. His two highlights were a grey wagtail in pool 1 and a great spotted woodpecker. Christine and I arrived early afternoon. As I walked up the central trail I flushed out a fox but didn't see it. Christine was watching from the hide and had a good view of it. I found a sparrowhawk's plucking post and a heap of thrush feathers. Further on was a fresh rabbit skin in the grass. A repeated 'pitchoo' call gave away the presence of a lovely marsh tit, a personal favourite of mine, which thankfully has become a regular occurrence in the reserve in recent times. Dragonflies showed well today: I noted at least two pairs of common darter tail-dipping (egg-laying) in central pool and a southern hawker patrolling by the hide. As we were leaving a couple of lesser whitethroats appeared in railway side bushes opposite the car park. This broke a disappointing record-less year for this species, particularly as it had been numerous in other localities.

On the afternoon of the 11th a grey heron took off from a pool, my first September record at the reserve. Also my best September for chiffchaffs.

October
Work on the 3rd involved removing fallen willows from the far

Shaggy ink-cap

end pool area that is at present dried out and quite safe to walk across. The willow branches, large and small, were gathered and sawn up. During these operations I discovered an old wren's nest in the bankside under tree roots, made chiefly of moss, leaves and feathers.

Two adult coots are still present, our first record of coots for October. Two goldcrests today accompanied a small tit flock around the reserve. Ten out of 28 goldcrest records for the reserve are from October.

During our rounds on the 3rd we noticed an abundance of fungi, including shaggy ink-caps, along the grassy start to the trail.

November
Sunday 7th Christine and I arrived to find the nature trail covered in a deep carpet of willow leaves that dampened our footsteps as we went round. Two coots remained. Surprise of the day was a drake teal that plopped down onto the water.

We were amused by a particularly tame robin that flitted around us as

we worked on the 21st, taking opportunities to grub hunt where we had churned up the pool edges with our boots. Our two wintering coots persevered with the disturbance, staying around pool 1. Long-tailed tits appeared as the work came to an end. Eight bird species noted without looking for any.

December
Two problems at present are hindering the smooth running of things. We have been burdened with the task of removing a three-seater sofa and armchair, recently dumped in our car park.

Secondly, two young local lads seem intent on making a nuisance of themselves in the reserve. Christopher caught them attempting to float a raft made from a wooden pallet on the far end pool and willow logs had been launched into the water.

To date 1993 is second only to 1988 for the number of bird species recorded at the reserve, May being the best month on record with 28 species, one ahead of May 1990 – clearly a good month to birdwatch at Broadway Gravel Pit.

A single elusive coot put in brief appearances on 24th and 30th making this record coot year complete, the species having been represented on site in every calendar month in 1993.

January 1994
Very good news is that the District Council have responded to my letter and taken away the rubbish that was dumped in the car park. As a follow

up to this I have prepared a new sign board for the car park which reads "DUMPING RUBBISH ON THIS SITE IS ILLEGAL. KEEP OUR COUNTRYSIDE CLEAN."

February
On the 6th we called in primarily to put up the new sign. The water level is indeed high, Christine waded with difficulty to footbridge 1 from trail marker 4. There was little to be seen.

Our bird species graph shows a disappointing start to the new year, lower than 1993 though higher than 1992 and 1991. I put the slow start down to the terrible weather conditions and a noticeable lack of tit flocks for other birds to follow.

March
At 6.00 p.m. on the 18th at least four fieldfares were present and I discovered someone had cut a bunch of daffodils from the embankment near the car park. Is nothing sacred? At this point I shut up the hide and left.

The 29th started beautiful and sunny, the sort of day you wish you could spend at the reserve instead of carrying on to work. I called in at 8.30 a.m. to check a report that garden rubbish had been dumped in our car park, despite my recent new "no tipping" sign. No sooner had I got out of the car than I was gladdened by song from within the reserve of a chiffchaff and a blackcap. Incidently this is our first March record for the latter species. Elsewhere around the reserve, wren, yellowhammer, dunnock, robin and bullfinch also sang. I found nine species of birds in two minutes without even leaving the car park.

Yellowhammer

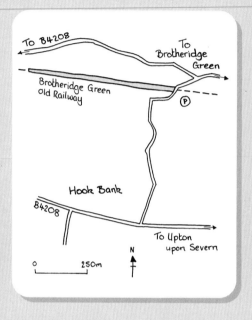
The Brotheridge Green Reserves

Brotheridge Green Old Railway, Melrose Farm Meadows, Boynes Coppice and Meadows and Drake Street Meadow. These reserves are all situated near the villages of Brotheridge Green and Welland, near Upton upon Severn.

Brotheridge Green Old Railway. The entrance is at the old bridge in Brotheridge Green at grid reference SO 817413, down steep steps. Park on the verges near the bridge. Open to Trust members carrying a membership card. Other visitors must first obtain a permit from the Trust's office.

Boynes Coppice and Meadows. Melrose Farm Meadows. Access to both sites is restricted and all visitors should first contact the Trust's office for a permit.

Drake Street Meadow. Because of its small size the meadow flora could easily be damaged by trampling during the spring and summer. Access is therefore restricted and visitors should first obtain a permit from the Trust's office. Otherwise you are welcome to lean on the gate and enjoy the flowers. The field gate is at grid reference SO 804398 by the side of the A4104 Upton upon Severn to Malvern road about 0.5 km east of Welland crossroads. This is a busy main road so please take care to park safely and to keep a look out for traffic.

Brotheridge Green Old Railway itself is part of the old dismantled Tewkesbury to Malvern railway line. It is about ½ mile long and 2 hectares in area, and lies about 2 miles west of Upton upon Severn. Soils are varied and support a wide range of plants. The reserve is particularly good for butterflies and for this it is a designated SSSI.

Melrose Farm Meadows. A 2 hectare reserve with hay meadows and a very old orchard.

Boynes Coppice and Meadows. This reserve consists of a small field of unimproved flower-rich pasture, three adjacent grass fields which are agriculturally improved and a small wood, now replanted with native broad-leaved trees.

Drake Street Meadow. A tiny meadow of less than ½ hectare by the A4104 at Welland.

Brotheridge Green Old Railway
by Rosalind Knowlson

It is a long time since Brotheridge Green saw steam engines puffing up and down its track, through the magnificent countryside, and under the stone bridge which crosses the reserve. Nowadays the railway has gone and in its place plants prosper. Grassland covers the old track-way and the embankments have been colonised by grassland, scrub, and young trees, giving a mosaic of habitat types.

Wood anemone

March 1993
With the sunshine warming my back I walked down the path on to the reserve. To my delight I saw little splashes of yellow primroses on the banks. Coupled with these and the surprisingly large amount of bird song it felt as if the wood spurges had burst forth to announce through their trumpet-shaped leaf formations that spring was finally on its way.

In the more wooded areas of the reserve wood anemones had started to flower. Their pure white petals fringed with delicate green leaves were set to carpet the bare ground beneath the still naked trees. Badgers have thrown their winter bedding out at the entrance of their setts.

"Spring is the season of colour, all the more arresting after the comparatively drab tones of winter."

April

Silver flowers breaking from the swelling buds of the goat willow; male oaks are starting to flower with little bells of yellow flowers; blackthorn flowers provide a splash of white.

Major nest building is occurring around the reserve by a variety of birds including robins, thrushes, sparrows, blue tits. Rooks in gale-tossed rookeries are settling down to incubate their eggs.

I always mark the swallows as a sign of spring and today I saw my first pair in flight across the reserve (11 April).

20 April: heard the song of the cuckoo, another signal that spring is truly here. The stems of the cowslips stand proud against the grassy banks.

May

"March is promise, May fulfilment." The hawthorns have a thick green covering of leaves and a mass of white blossom on the way.

At the far end of the reserve there is the familiar musky odour and considerable evidence of badger digging and communal latrines, and the unmistakable badger trails which tend to go through fences, hedges and scrub rather than round them!

Early this month when there was good sunshine I saw a small group of speckled wood butterflies in the far glade and one lone orange-tip resting on cow parsley.

June

Brotheridge Green has exploded into life and colour, with flowers jostling for position between the tall grasses. Butterflies are abundant and there is bird song in every tree.

As many as 17 speckled woods were seen, with five orange-tips, four brimstones, one small tortoiseshell and one large white.

The track's green carpet is set ablaze with the yellow of the buttercups, the white flowers of the greater stitchwort, the pinks of the herb-Robert, the blues of the forget-me-nots, and the multitude of colours of the vetches.

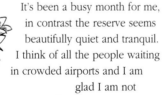

Bramble

July

"The month of changing colours." The butterflies seem to be taking full advantage of the sunshine and the abundant nectar supply. Saw two peacocks and a brief glimpse of what looked like a pair of large skippers as well as a group of ringlets.

The jewel in the crown this month must be the delicate purple-headed clustered bellflower – a plant of limy grasslands now all too few in the county.

August

It's been a busy month for me, in contrast the reserve seems beautifully quiet and tranquil. I think of all the people waiting in crowded airports and I am glad I am not among them. I am here quietly watching the birds and their young fly by.

The reserve still seems green, although a lot of the tall grasses appear almost like a hay meadow ready for harvest. The late summer plants add their own touch of colour to the scene, such as hawkweed oxtongue.

Clustered bellflower

September

"Let the battle commence." Every year at Brotheridge Green the grass is cut and the scrub and brambles cut back and kept in check and all the glades are cut and cleared.

To minimise the disturbance of all this work, only one side of the track is cut, alternating from side to side each year. Although a tractor could complete this work in no time at all, there is no access for large machinery and so an army of volunteers, myself included, must toil away under a hot sun with machetes, brush cutters, rakes and pitch-forks.

Sunday 26 September: all grass raked off and remaining glades cut and cleared. The long grass and brambles were piled up as in old style hay making and then bonfires were lighted and stoked with grass. Myself and an army of wonderful volunteers lie back exhausted and watch the sun set over Brotheridge Green. We looked at the work we had achieved with pride.

With the smoke rising from the bonfires it almost looked as if the steam engines of long ago had returned.

October

"The month of the trees." This is the month when the greatest number of the trees reach their full autumn glory. The reserve has all the shades of autumn: golds, reds, bronze and yellows; in contrast the ferns on the banks seem an extra brilliant green.

15 October: heavy frost. The grasses and leaves crack under foot. The leaves on the banks are individually edged with frost. The remaining spiders' webs look magical

as every drop of dew is turned to ice. Even the bird song seems quiet this frosty morning.

November

The bare branches of the trees and shrubs seem naked in the autumn cold. All of them are stripped of their leaves and we can see once more the true shape of the elm, elder, willow, walnut, ash, and beech, with their patterns of trunk and branches and twigs etched boldly against the sky.

Hazel catkins promise in no uncertain way the fulfilment that must be deferred until spring. As if to complete this winter scene, snow falls but does not settle.

December

It is winter at Brotheridge Green, the ground is sodden under foot and the cleared glades and track show no signs of re-growth.

The soft shield-ferns' and male-ferns' green leaves contrast with the dark earth under the trees on the banks. The umbellifers stand with the dead stems still upright.

Bird boxes have fallen off their trees and so must be taken down for repair. Tree felling has been carried out this month to give greater light on to the reserve. Red berries on the hawthorns add colour to the scene.

January 1994

Buds on oak, beech and ash start to swell. Puffed up against the cold, a red-breasted robin alighted briefly between his search of garden bird tables. Gangs of blue tits visit Brotheridge Green; their main source of food is not found here but in neighbouring gardens.

The track-way is still very boggy and waterlogged under foot. Despite the cold I walked the full length of the reserve and saw an increasing number of badger and rabbit signs. Brotheridge Green becomes Brotheridge water meadow and the birds enjoy a bath.

February

The snowdrops are pushing their delicate heads through the banks of grass and leaf litter and give a glimpse of what spring will have to offer. A few clusters of primroses provide another splash of colour. The sun filtered through giving that first feeling that spring is on its way.

Badgers are out and about, and diggings for worms, scrapes and communal latrines are much in evidence. Checked on the badger setts and all looks well, lots of fresh

earth and bedding piled at the entrance. Well worn paths are much in evidence, pressed smooth by many pads.

22 February: one inch of snow fell, transforming the muddy track into a white wonderland, if only for the day.

March

Drizzling rain, hawthorn is in leaf giving a green covering to the lower shrub community of Brotheridge Green. Treecreepers out and about with the robins, wrens, blue tits and a woodpecker. The hazels are carrying their lambs' tails varying in colour from light green to gold.

April

The birds at Brotheridge Green have been busy and nest building in the trees has started once again. The hawthorn is in full leaf and blossoms are on the way. The yellow petals of the cowslips and the white stitchworts are in flower. The garlic mustard emits its smell, and shows its flowers.

The badger tracks are still very much in constant use. If they ever come to rename this site it should surely be Badgeridge Green.

Melrose Farm Meadows
by Linda Lewis

These two small traditionally farmed hay meadows and one very old orchard are situated on the edge of what was, until the Enclosures, Hook Common in ancient Malvern Chase. Adjoining the orchard is a small area of trees and scrub, originally the garden of on old cottage. This provides shelter and cover for birds, mammals and a variety of insect life.

The meadows, originally part of Melrose Farm, have been in the possession of the same family since the 1830s. In 1976, they were purchased by the Worcestershire Nature Conservation Trust. Having watched the meadows change with each season for 78 years, I gladly agreed to continue to care for them, thus leaving unbroken my, and my family's, life-long connection with them.

The Trust carries out any necessary maintenance in December, January and February before spring growth starts, or at other times if an emergency arises. No ploughing takes place, neither are artificial fertilisers, insecticides or herbicides used.

In July the grass is mown and any fruit picking takes place before the meadows are grazed until about November. We now reap the benefit of this management routine, for from the end of February we are rewarded with a wealth of flowers and grasses.

From late February and into March, the primroses, cuckooflowers and violets appear, and under the hedgerow is a haze of bluebells. Cowslips follow, including one clump of false oxlip, which has bloomed each year in the same position for at least 90 years.

Before the cowslips fade in May, the orchard is literally taken over by green-winged orchids in shades of pink, white, maroon and lovely bi-colours. These Tom Thumbs, as country people used to call them, have increased rapidly, and have spread into the two small meadows.

In 1993, the first spotted-orchid was found in Melrose meadows, a cause for celebration indeed. Space does not permit a list of all the flowers, but we must mention the meadow saffron, ragged-Robin, saw-wort, betony, yellow-rattle, lady's bedstraw, pepper-saxifrage, devils'-bit scabious and dyer's greenweed, not forgetting the splendid display of much-loved buttercups.

These flowers of ancient pastures, together with a large variety of grasses, support the many species of moths, butterflies and other insects, including an occasional glow-worm, which inhabit these lovely meadows.

The tall hedges provide valuable winter food for birds such as fieldfares and redwings, which arrive from November onwards. Sadly there are fewer birds seen on the reserve

now, and we no longer hear nightingales or grasshopper warblers. A plus are the wrens and the long-tailed tits which have increased, but so have the magpies!

Badgers regularly trek through the meadows on their nightly jaunts, and are particularly fond of the fallen apples and damsons.

Representatives of English Nature visit the meadows from time to time, and all agree, that for its size, this reserve is a marvellous example of old English pastures.

In 1991, David Woodfall, a nature photographer, received a request from the Royal Society for Nature Conservation to submit photographs of an old English meadow, with cowslips, green-winged orchids and trees in blossom. He contacted Worcestershire Nature Conservation Trust, who suggested he tried Melrose.

Two of these photographs were selected to be enlarged and framed and signed by David Attenborough. It was a surprise to receive a print of Melrose meadows together with a letter of thanks from the RSNC. We regard this as a reward for all the care and work put into these meadows over the many years, and also a reward for the village, of which they are a part, and which has remained almost unaltered for over 100 years.

Dyer's greenweed

Adder's-tongue

Boynes Coppice and Meadows

The small field of old pasture has a rich flora with over 60 vascular

plants recorded. There are many green-winged orchids, and other uncommon plants include adder's-tongue fern, dyer's greenweed, pepper-saxifrage and pale sedge. The larger fields are generally less rich having been partially 'improved' in the recent past by the use of pesticides and fertilisers. These fields are gradually developing a richer flora under traditional management. All the fields are put-up for hay during the summer and grazed in autumn and early winter.

Boynes Coppice is said to have originally been planted in the 19th century to screen the now-dismantled railway from Boynes House to the north. The reserve is good for insects including small copper and common blue butterflies, meadow grasshoppers, speckled bush-cricket and dark bush-cricket.

Drake Street Meadow

This small meadow on Keuper Marl clays is divided into two sections by a central ditched stream. The meadow slopes down to the stream and the slopes are thickly carpeted with cowslips, with smaller numbers of green-winged orchids, burnet- and pepper-saxifrages, and adder's-tongue fern. The ground flora of the southern hedge contains some woodland species, notably bluebells, goldilocks, dog's mercury, primroses, and both wood dog-violets, and is perhaps a relic of an old woodland.

Chance Wood

Chance Wood lies about 2 miles north of the Worcestershire border in Staffordshire between Stourton and Kinver. It is a 3 hectare planted woodland given to the Trust in 1977.

The reserve may be visited at any time. Access is via a bridleway running south from the main Stourbridge to Bridgnorth road (A458), about 800 m west of a junction with the A449. Parking is very restricted, with a little space on nearby road verges. Please take care as the main road is heavy with traffic. The bridleway starts immediately west of the small Post Office at grid reference SO 845859. After about 200 m enter the reserve on the right. The bridleway continues round the reserve and footpaths may be followed to Kinver.

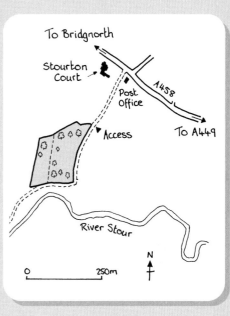

Planted as an ornamental wood last century, Chance Wood is dominated by large oaks and beech, with specimens of hornbeam, ash, sycamore, horse-chestnut, sweet chestnut and a few conifers. It is an open woodland situated on a hillside overlooking the River Stour. A dry valley runs through the reserve and down to the river.

The underlying well-drained Bunter pebble-beds and sandstones have produced dry, rather acid soils which suit plants such as wood sage and foxglove, though the ground flora is not rich in species numbers. There are areas of planted rhododendrons and azaleas. In spring extensive carpets of snowdrops pushing through carpets of dead leaves are a striking feature, and there are some bluebells. Other interesting plants are dame's-violet and Italian lords-and-ladies, a relative of wild arum with dark green leaves and palely marked veins. Both are garden escapes which have become naturalised.

The big trees and old timber are good for many woodland birds. Tits, woodpeckers, nuthatches and treecreepers are frequent. The old trees provide a good supply of invertebrate food and contain many suitable nesting holes, supplemented with nest boxes for birds and with bat boxes. The close association with the low-lying Stour valley and its patches of willows, scrub, trees and rank vegetation makes the whole area rich in bird life. The river itself drains from the Black Country and although it is highly polluted kingfishers are sometimes seen.

Stacks of dead and slowly decaying wood from tree felling have been left in some places and these are good sites for fungi and invertebrates. The large ichneumon fly *Rhyssa persuasoria* has been seen egg-laying, inserting its long ovipositor deep into timber, thus parasitising the larvae of the wood-wasp *Uroceras gigas*. These insects are uncommon and are found in old woodland.

A romantic feature of Chance Wood is a small cemetery for dogs on the hill-top with headstones dating back to 1869: who was "Punch, died 1898"?

Ichneumon fly

33

A YEAR IN THE LIFE OF Christopher Cadbury Wetland Reserve, Upton Warren

This reserve is in two parts, the northern 17 hectares of Moors Pool and its surrounding marshes and grasslands, and the southern 10 hectares of the Flash Pools and adjacent grasslands. It is an SSSI and lies by the A38 at Upton Warren between Droitwich and Bromsgrove.

The entrance to the Moors Pool is at grid reference SO 936677 on the A38(T) Droitwich to Bromsgrove road adjacent to the AA phone box about 450 m north of the Swan Inn at Upton Warren. A track leads across a field to a small car park. Access to the Flash Pools is from the sailing centre car park about 200 m south-west of the Swan Inn at grid reference SO 932673. Then walk round the south-west bank of the sailing pool. The sailing pool and its car park are not part of the reserve. A small part of this car park may be used by Trust members on weekdays up to about 4.30 p.m. Please use the paths to the bird-watching hides and do not stray from them as this disturbs the birds. The reserve is open at any time to members of the Trust carrying membership cards. Non-members must obtain a permit to visit from the Trust's office. The A38(T) is an extremely busy main road. Take care when entering the reserve.

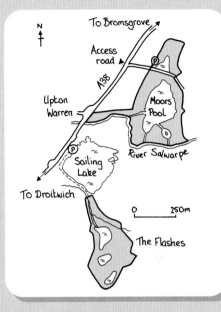

by Alan Shepherd

The existence of this reserve owes much to Christopher Cadbury who made the original land purchase in 1968 for the Royal Society for Nature Conservation so it could be managed by the Trust on a long-term lease. He has generously helped to pay for many developments and improvements on the reserve, which now bears his name as a small token of our recognition and appreciation of his work.

Sabine's gull

The reserve is very good for birds, with a total species list of 220. Virtually any species can turn-up: American waders, unusual warblers, unexpected birds of prey, surprising ducks and rare gulls, as well as the commoner breeding and wintering species.

March 1993

Sand martins are usually the first summer immigrants to arrive back. The first of the breeding birds arrives on the mud in the shape of little ringed plovers, but real spring arrives to the tune of the willow warbler, typically at the very end of the month, although its close relative the chiffchaff may be singing somewhat less tunefully a few days earlier.

Brimstone butterflies emerge on the first sunny day, soon followed by peacock and small tortoiseshell and finally by the ragged-winged comma. Supplies of nectar are scarce as few plants are in flower but somehow these seemingly fragile insects manage to survive and lay their eggs to ensure a second flight in summer.

Back on the pool margins black-tailed godwits and oystercatchers are usually seen before the month is out. Along the River Salwarpe butterbur begins to flower surrounded by lesser celandines, and the blackthorn flowers often herald a short cold snap: the 'blackthorn winter' when some early migrants return a part-way south to find insect food.

April

Visitors to the Flash Pools this month may be surprised to see the distant dandelions around the Sailing Pool moving! Raising their binoculars they see the first yellow wagtails of the year running amongst the brilliant yellow dandelion flowers on the close cropped grass, accompanied by the resident pied wagtails.

Spring passage begins in earnest with the arrival of the first swallows and house martins, followed on successive days by sedge warblers (many stay to breed), redstarts, common sandpipers, greenshanks, dunlins, whinchats and common terns. All of these move on to breed elsewhere, although the common terns had a surprise in store this year. These birds appear briefly in this little corner of Worcestershire to feed and strengthen themselves for the further journey, sometimes as far as the Arctic Circle. I like to explain it to visitors as the equivalent to a stop at the motorway services for a plate of egg and chips on the way to holiday destination. But it is more important than that to birds. We play temporary host to birds which move between continents, and as such we can affect things on a global scale.

Although protected nationally and disappearing at an alarming rate, due mainly to loss of suitable breeding ponds, the great crested newt is still quite common in this area. Smooth newts also occur but both species are difficult to find unless one knows their typical hiding places.

May
'Always expect the unexpected'

Common tern

seem to be the watch-words, proved in one week by a sanderling frightened off by an osprey, followed by records of little stint, curlew sandpiper and bar-tailed godwit on successive days, the climax being Worcestershire's first ever record of white stork! Many of these birds are attracted to the Flashes by its resemblance to an estuary: the large expanse of bare mud must promise good feeding to a tired and hungry wader. I must mention the importance of the Flashes as a unique habitat within the county. The very existence of the pools is due to the presence of salt in the Droitwich area. The extraction of salt from underground brine lakes led to the slumping of the fields and subsequent flooding to form pools. Around pool margins are the typical salt-tolerant plants of the area, such as the lesser sea-spurrey which carpets the wetter patches of mud, accompanied by the spear-leaved (or hastate) orache and reflexed saltmarsh-grass.

June
After the mad rush of May the reserve falls into a relative calm as most species settle down to breed. The occasional late wader on its way to the Arctic may drop in, this year a sanderling, but there are plenty of resident species to see. On the Flashes, little ringed plovers attempt to breed, scraping their meagre nest saucers on the gravel patches. These nests, though

Little ringed plover

superbly camouflaged, are still easy pickings to the local moorhens and coots, both of which will take the eggs, as will magpies, crows and foxes. In 1990 we attempted protection by placing wire cages over the nests after the laying of the second egg. The instinct to sit and incubate is so strong that it takes a mere 15 minutes before the disturbed parent is back on the nest and brooding. Moorhens actually stand on the cages trying to gain access, but the small mesh ensures that nothing larger than the parents can get through.

Away from the birds, it is quite easy to see eight species of dragonflies and damselflies in a single day. For the butterfly enthusiast the Salwarpe Path walk is a must at the end of the month, when white-letter hairstreaks appear around the elms and wych elms, descending to feed on the thistle flowers in the rough 'meadow'. Numbers of common blues, large skippers and ringlets also occur.

We are attempting at the Cristopher Cadbury Reserve to recreate some wet grasslands and marshy areas by managing the water levels with a system of sluices. Closing the sluices in late autumn retains the winter rainfall to benefit the wintering wildfowl, and the higher spring levels which result provide more breeding sites for great crested grebes, little grebes, coots and ducks. The natural evaporation then leaves damp areas for waders such as lapwings to nest in the shorter grass and wet areas provide more insect food for the chicks.

One of the more exciting developments in recent years has come about as a result of a few keen volunteers providing nesting facilities for common terns. In 1991 the first-ever breeding in Worcestershire took place on a purpose-built artificial island in the Moors Pool. Unfortunately, the single chick to hatch died of a liver defect, but this year the terns attempted to breed again. This time, a Canada goose trampled on the eggs but we live in hope that soon they will succeed in fledging young and establishing a colony. [A pair bred successfully in 1994.]

July

The reedbeds at the reserve during this month seethe with activity as reed warblers busily feed their young. They build their elaborate nests suspended amongst the reeds and by July some of them are caring for a second brood, foraging on the reed stems and leaves for aphids or flying to the nearby willows to hunt for flies and caterpillars. Some may be feeding cuckoo chicks although this parasitic summer visitor seems to be less common nowadays.

On the water, broods of tufted ducks are seen diving frantically for food, shepherded by their ever-alert mothers, and young great crested and little grebes ride on their parent's backs while waxing fat on a diet of sticklebacks.

Tufted duck

August

A busy month, with up to 110 bird species possible. Spotted redshanks, ruffs and greenshanks feed on invertebrates in the mud. Black terns

hawk for insects over the pool. This year brought a black-necked grebe to the Moors Pool. Indeed, this is historically the most likely month for a rarity to turn up. Observers scan the gull roost for less common species like this year's Mediterranean gull, whilst inwardly hoping for something as rare as 1988's least sandpiper, then only the third record of this tiny American wader in Britain.

Hobbies hunt over the Moors Pool for the numerous dragonflies. This fast-flying little falcon tends to come north from breeding places in southern England on the heels of the swallow flocks and it is even agile enough to take bats or swifts. All of the swifts are gone by now, but pipistrelle, Daubenton's and noctule bats all fly over the reserve in the gathering dusk.

Big event of 1993: at a ringing session on 8 August the first burst of song from the Cetti's warbler was heard. The bird stayed for the winter at the Moors Pool and eventually sired the first ever recorded brood of Cetti's warbler in Worcestershire.

September

Ducks begin to moult out of eclipse plumage and become easier to distinguish. The mud uncovered by the lower water levels around the Moors Pool was quickly colonised by amphibious bistort, celery-leaved buttercup and other rapid growers. Ruffs, dunlins, little stints and curlew sandpipers all exploited the wide muddy margins.

Hobby

One of the highlights for three lucky observers was the year's third overflying osprey, seen as they were repairing a handrail on a hide.

October

The big event of this month was the arrival of the NRA with machinery at the Broad Meadow. This large area of unexciting grassland was to be transformed into a series of pools, scrapes and ditches, flooded in winter but revealed as breeding and feeding areas during summer and autumn under the water level management regime. Heavy earth-movers shifted 3,000 tonnes of topsoil, putting some out into the pool to create islands. The dam was repaired to enable us to control the water level more accurately, and high spoil banks around the Broad Meadow Pool were levelled to make viewing easier. One of the islands received a topping of 40 tonnes of shingle to make it attractive to terns and little ringed plovers. All this work took the best part of the month to complete and was a collaborative project between the NRA and the Trust based on ideas formulated by the reserve management committee and agreed by English Nature: a prime example of all pulling together to benefit wildlife conservation.

The feeding station at the Flashes swings into action at the end of October, drawing in flocks of passerines from all around to the £400's-worth of food provided by the volunteer fund-raisers. This facility is probably the best place in

the entire country to see water rails, normally only glimpsed briefly skulking through the reedbeds or even more often only heard giving its eerie grunts and squeals from deep wet cover. The food spilt on the ground proves an irresistible draw as do the small birds which frequently fall victim to this unsuspected predator.

November

Four bearded tits appeared as a reward for the late-stayers at a work party day, perhaps a just reward for a long day of physical effort. Goldeneye on the Moors Pool join the large numbers of pochard, tufted and other duck. Ruddy ducks have departed by now but shoveler occur in nationally important numbers, swirling around in close circles as they sift the seeds

of the amphibious bistort through their outsize bills.

December

This is the quietest month in the reserve calendar with most plants and insects dead or dormant. Small mammals can be seen crossing open patches of ground but generally birds dominate yet again.

The Flash Pools are actually more saline than seawater but due to their shallowness they freeze over quickly, forcing most wildfowl to move to larger waters. The Moors Pool remains open longer due to its size, and small groups of ducks are often seen huddled around the last remaining open water. This year, the arrival of nine white-fronted geese from their breeding grounds in arctic Russia heralded the onset of winter proper. The last abiding memory of

1993 was a tawny owl calling at 11.50 p.m. to send the senior warden and his wife home from a New Year Party.

January 1994

There is always a tendency at a wetland reserve to watch the water and its edges for signs of wintering wildfowl, this year including wigeon, shelduck and dunlin among the more common species of mallard, Canada goose, gadwall, tufted duck, and pochard. Above the pools the air is thick with fieldfare and redwing flocks, and siskins and redpolls feed in the alders. Birds of prey include kestrel, sparrowhawks and peregrine all in the air together – a sight impossible to see a few years ago.

February

Last year there was an influx of

shags into the Midlands in the wake of the pollution from the Braer disaster, but thankfully nothing so drastic occurred this year. A small rise in numbers of great crested grebes promised a taste of warmer weather to come as they began to pair up and to perform their ritualised mating displays.

Many of the human contingent were engaged in their own winter pursuits, for this is the season of the work party ... the first Sunday in every month from October to April sees a varied crew of workers hard at the task of maintaining and in many cases improving the reserve. Fencing, reed cutting, tree planting, building screens from reeds, pollarding willows and alders along the Salwarpe, and keeping paths clear, are all routine jobs to be fitted into the short working period granted by the absence of any breeding wildlife. There are even a few retired folks who willingly give up an odd weekday to help with urgent tasks such as clearing fallen trees from the brook, not an inviting prospect on an ice-bound foggy morning! It is never possible to thank these dedicated helpers enough, as without them the wardens' job would be well-nigh impossible.

March

March 1994 saw the biggest event for some years with the opening of a brand new tower hide overlooking the Moors Pool and Amy's Marsh. A small ceremony to open the hide and to dedicate the new marsh to Amy Calvert was held on 10 March. Amy was a lover of nature at an early age but tragically died aged only three. Her grandfather oversaw the work on the site and we were pleased to be able to commemorate her in this way.

The new hide marks the beginning of a new phase in the development of the reserve. We now have viewing facilities to match those of any local reserve, and these complement the varied habitats which has developed or been created over the last 25 years under the Trust's ownership. While there is little scope for expansion, we can maximise what we have for wildlife, and provide access for people to see it. The hides of 25 years ago can no longer cope with the numbers of people who flock to enjoy and appreciate what is sadly now just a small remnant of the wetlands that have gone. We have to preserve and enhance what remains and hope that agricultural changes and economic pressures become less damaging.

Cleeve Prior

This 11½ hectare site is managed by the Trust under an Agreement with Hereford and Worcester County Council. It lies on a hillside overlooking the River Avon, part of a west-facing scarp slope which also includes Windmill Hill reserve about ½ mile to the south. The steep slopes are covered with woodland and scrub, with a narrow band of grassland along part of the bridleway at the top of the hillside. Deadly nightshade grows on this reserve. Up to 2 m tall with tubular brownish purple or bluish flowers it is a poisonous plant bearing luscious black berries 1–2 cm in diameter. Visitors should not touch the plant and must take special care to ensure children do not eat the berries. If berries are eaten seek medical assistance immediately.

This reserve is about 4½ miles north-east of Evesham adjacent to the village of Cleeve Prior on the left bank of the River Avon. Access is at grid reference SP 079496 from Mill Lane. This lane is the first turning left for northbound traffic entering Cleeve Prior village on the B4085. Limited roadside parking in Mill Lane.

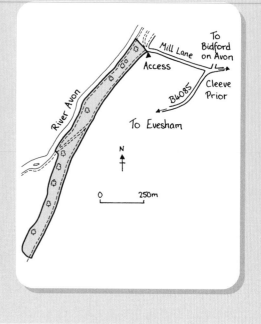

by Bob Woodroofe

April 1993

Good news! The reserve has been accepted into the Countryside Commission's Countryside Stewardship scheme, providing funding for bridleway clearance and hedge-cutting.

The annual weekly Butterfly Monitoring Scheme walks have started and will continue until September. We record butterflies to study the effects of the various kinds of management on their numbers.

May

Many of the more common flowers are now coming into bloom. Swallows, cuckoos and warblers have returned.

Down by the river many alderflies with their wings folded over their backs like a miniature roof. Butterflies seen this month include speckled wood, orange-tip and holly blue. The woodland contains much fallen timber, deliberately left as a haven for all sorts of creatures: snails, millipedes, woodlice, beetles and many different kinds of fungi.

June

The reserve speciality, deadly nightshade, is in flower. It is about a metre high, with dull purple-green, brownish or bluish flowers. Only a few specimens are scattered around in shady sites. Beware their poisonous berries later in the year.

Deadly nightshade

Down by the river patches of Himalayan balsam with its purple flowers and explosive seed capsules have invaded along the bank. There is lots of wildlife on the bank-side vegetation: yellow-green spiders with long front-pointing legs, red cardinal beetles, amber snails on the reeds.

July

On 3 July I showed a party from the Trust's Bromsgrove Group around the reserve. Highlights were clouds of marbled whites and ringlet butterflies, and a few commas and red admirals. Plants included pyramidal and bee orchids, deadly nightshade and ploughman's-spikenard, and a lively common shrew was running along the bridleway.

August

Yellow water-lily in flower at the riverside, and also the small white flowers of arrowhead: notice the triangular pointed leaves from which it takes its name.

Both the small and large white butterflies are now common, and brimstone, red admiral, peacock and small tortoiseshells are feeding on the thistle flowers. Skippers also on view with their buzzing moth-like flight. Found a bright green female oak bush cricket with very long antennae and a wicked-looking curved ovipositor.

Brimstone

Highlight of the month: a hobby played cat and mouse with a flock of house martins above the reserve! I'm not sure who was chasing who!

September

The first shades of autumn yellows and golds are beginning to show on the leaves. Ivy is in flower and humming with insects: flies, bees and wasps. Speckled woods are still found in the dappled light along the hedgerow. Also another small brown butterfly: could it possibly be a brown hairstreak? Goldfinch flocks are on the thistle heads and squirrels are nutting on the hazels.

October

The reserve was opened on 17 October ten years ago by Lord Peter Melchett, so I thought I would walk round on the same date.

A cold frosty morning, still October air, clear blue sky. Grass silvery white with frost crunches

under your feet. Pale sunshine gleams through the trees leaving long shadows. Russet and gold shades of autumn light the old bridleway, a tree-lined track where once Romans marched, now rutted by horseshoes with thin ice on the puddles. No wind: stop, look, listen. So quiet you can hear the leaves fall, pitter-patter to the ground, almost like rain.

November

Wild grey November day, wind blasting through the trees, cold and sharp. Wonderful natural roaring sound of the wind, like rushing water or a train in the distance. It has rained heavily, the bridleway is sodden, squelching underfoot. The leaves, stripped from the trees, lie like a carpet along the path. The hedge, draped with the silvery grey seed-heads of traveller's-joy, glows red with haws, over which fieldfares and redwings jostle. A splash of yellow in the grass, a late lone buttercup struggling to flower.

December

Work parties cleared the undergrowth on the drift road down to the river, to make walking easier, as it gets very slippy in winter. The holly tree in the hedge suffered a 'severe pruning' by persons unknown, presumably Christmas sales.

January 1994

At the bottom of the drift road I notice some large birds in one of the

ash trees on the river bank in Pickersham Meadow. What are they? As I creep closer they become clearer, outlined against the blue sky. I can't believe it, four jet black cormorants, they look so out of place in a tree! Nowadays more are moving inland to become pests on fish farms. I wonder if the Birmingham Anglers Association know they are next door to the recently stocked fishing lake!

I struggle up the sloping path to the top of the escarpment. Judging by the slide marks down the bank where their runs are, the badgers have as much trouble as I do.

February

There is a rumble and roar from across the river. A plume of blue smoke, a funeral pyre of hedgerows and trees. The diggers have moved in, carving the new Norton Lenchwick bypass through the meadows. A brown gaping wound across the beautiful green fields. What madness and for what? To get from A to B faster, then where? At a cost to the tax-payer of nineteen million pounds, what if we spent this on conservation instead!

March

A year in the life of the Cleeve Prior reserve has flown by, the Silver Jubilee year has come and gone. It has been a good one with many interesting developments on the reserve, much accomplished, much seen and enjoyed. A new year lies ahead with new challenges. We will continue to gradually develop the reserve and maintain the diversity of habitats and flora and fauna for us all to enjoy!

Goldfinch

The Devil's Spittleful and Rifle Range

The 25 hectares of the Devil's Spittleful reserve belong to the Trust. The adjacent 36 hectares, the Rifle Range, belong to the Wyre Forest District Council and are managed by the Trust under an Agreement. Both reserves are SSSIs. The reserves are on the western edge of Kidderminster. This site is one of the few extensive areas of heathland remaining in Worcestershire, and is important in a national context. The light sandy soils support an interesting and unusual set of plants and animals typical of free-draining, somewhat acid soils. Most of the reserve is fairly flat but for the rocky sandstone knoll crowned with planted Scots pines.

The reserves can be visited at any time and can be reached on foot from A456 Kidderminster to Bewdley road via Sandy Lane, a track running southwards immediately east of the entrance to the West Midland Safari Park at grid reference SO 807759. There is also access at the west end of Rifle Range Road at SO 815752. These reserves are especially prone to damage by fires. Please take special care not to discard cigarettes, matches or other combustible material.

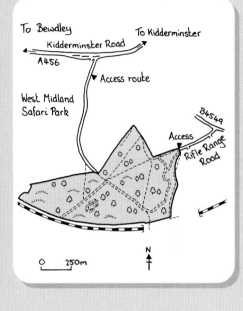

by Dave Scott

March and April 1993

Ruby tiger moth caterpillar, the dark blackish form, (both this and light fawn form are found here) on heather after hibernation, oak eggar moth caterpillar in broom, emperor moth cocoon in heather (smaller ones are males), green tiger beetle running and flying amongst heather and on sandy paths. In March the male orange underwing moths fly in sunshine mostly fairly high around birches: they look entirely orange-brown when in flight. A few holly blue and orange-tip butterflies seen in April: both species uncommon on the reserve.

Green tiger beetle

European gorse flowering well at this time of year, conspicuously yellow – good quantities in relatively limited areas of reserves. Spring whitlowgrass flowering here and there in stony places in March. A single twayblade, not yet in flower, noted under trees on the eastern side of the Rifle Range, far from the Devil's Spittleful (western) area where they are usually seen.

Common dog-violets coming into flower, mostly in scrub and woodland areas.

Woodcock roding display flight 6.30 p.m. 7 March – quite an early date. Seen fairly commonly at dusk until end of June or so; song thrush and skylark singing 18 March and by 16 April much song heard – skylarks sing

mainly from, and nest on, neighbouring farmland. Redpoll flocks (20–30) on 16 and 29 March; chiffchaff seen 18 March, singing on 24 March, willow warbler 7 April, whitethroat 21 April, grey partridge on 8 and 15 April. Both species of partridge breed on the reserve and on neighbouring farmland – as elsewhere grey partridge have decreased. Tree pipits on 6 April.

May, June and July

Day-flying common heath moths fluttering over heather (here normally small dark heathland form, rather than larger yellower form most often found on limestone). Speckled yellow moths especially along paths and glades in wooded patches, green tiger beetle in May. Gorse shield-bugs (yellow line round edges – well camouflaged as gorse seeds) out of hibernation. A snake-fly (much scarcer here than related scorpion fly), sloe bugs, three parent bugs with their batches of pale green eggs on birch 26 May – not a species I see here often in spite of its liking for birch.

Small heath and small copper butterflies fairly typical of acid grassland and heath. Male brimstone butterfly 24 May (not common on reserve), common blues, long-horn moths *Adela reaumurella* dancing in little clouds round bushes and branches and smaller number of the bigger Degeer's longhorn *Nemophora degeerella*. 24 May longhorn moth *Nemapotogon swammerdamella* (name much bigger than the moth). Male fox moth disturbed into flight 25 May at 2.30 p.m., a typical day-flyer of heath and moorland – natural flight times seem to be 4 p.m. to 7 or 8 p.m.

Green hairstreak butterflies 19 and 25 May – reasonably common most years since 1985/1986 – before this no records apparently! 24 May *Pyla fusca* pyralid moth, flying round heather only burnt on 18 May. Marvellously camouflaged little moth – charcoal grey against burnt heather. It lays its eggs on burnt heather stems and the larvae feed on burnt stems and the new growth. It appears magically round burnt patches of heather. How long did it take to evolve such habits?

By June large skipper butterflies, and also grass wave moths, another heathland species with larvae feeding on heathers, disturbed into day flying and many more flying at night. A single small pearl-bordered fritillary

Small heath

noted on 30 June is quite unusual here. Both pearl-bordered and small pearl-bordered fritillaries occur in ones and twos, but not every year.

By 27 July small heath's second brood out, and by 5 July meadow browns and ringlets. Ringlets were virtually unrecorded (apart from a single specimen in 1976) until 1984 when they appeared in reasonable numbers and have been here ever since. Common blue damselfly 28 July, also second brood holly blues, oak eggar moths flying late afternoon, and speedwell plume moth *Stenoptilia pterodactyla*. Hornets nest found high in a dead birch, a first for the reserve though hornets seen here in some years.

Shepherd's cress flowering in a white haze over the eastern end of the 'horse-fields', where heavier grazing (by two highland cattle and a cross) has produced a much finer vegetation with much exposed sand beloved of this cress. Also a better than usual crop of our tiny but fascinating sand-loving spring vetch, and both changing and early forget-me-not which enjoy a similar habitat. In the acid grassland of these fields there are also gems of wild pansy (or heart's-ease) and heath dog-violets coming into flower. Heath dog-violets do appear to have 'read the book' and on the whole appear in heath or grassland, leaving the rest to common dog-violets, though some I am convinced are hybrids.

Buck's-horn plantain, annual knawel, both also tiny sand lovers, appear along on a few tracks and paths, and the tiny pinky-mauve sand spurrey opens in the sunshine. Like buck's-horn plantain it relishes the trampling of feet, which produces the near-bare ground conditions it likes. Bird's-foot, a tiny but fascinating vetch which has cream flowers with delicate pinkish bee guides, is common in the sandy grassland and heathland. It is a rarity away from the sand. Heath groundsel in sandy places, usually after disturbance, sheep's-bit and harebells flowering in the heathland.

Occasional meadow saxifrage plants in the grassland on the south-west corner, but luxuriating in a brilliant white band at the edges of the railway ballast along the Severn Valley Railway adjoining the reserve. The latin name *Saxifraga* means stone-breaker, and from observations here and elsewhere it seemes to like growing on stony ground or even in cracks on solid sandstone. Heath speedwell flowers in the grassy areas and viper's bugloss produces a splash of colour around the reserve and on the Severn Valley Railway near the Kidderminster tunnel, probably much encouraged by the dumping of sand from parts of the railway further east.

Harebell

A few spikes of ploughman's-spikenard (three this year) put in a strange appearance as a lime-loving plant in an acidic heathland, growing on a small crumbling ridge of concrete, presumably still containing traces of lime, left over from the site's military past.

Like a neat stitchwort the field mouse-ear shows white blooms along the edges of paths, mostly in sandy ground scattered on both east and west sides of the reserve. Nationally this plant has a rather easterly distribution.

Redstart singing round Spadeful Rock on 9 May but probably did not breed here, and a wood warbler which probably did. Tree pipits singing 5 May. Woodcock roding at 5 a.m. on dawn chorus walk, cuckoo calling 14 May and garden warbler and blackcaps on 16 May. On 17 June both turtle dove and lesser whitethroat sang in the hawthorn-infested but interesting grassland on eastern edge of the reserve. Also green woodpeckers (common on reserve) and sparrowhawks which nest most years either on reserve or in nearby Whitehill Wood.

A large grass snake on 25 May – not infrequently seen on the reserve but why never any adders? Adders also not found in similar habitat at Hartlebury Common, and yet in Wyre Forest, nearby to the west, in Habberley Valley only a few miles north, and near Kinver and Kingsford they are quite common.

August and September

Silver-washed fritillary on 4 August. A small breeding population is present each year centred around the Spadeful Rock and woodland to west and north. An orange-warted full-grown emperor moth caterpillar on heather. This is a characteristic species of heath and moorland and the caterpillar may have pink, white, yellow or orange warts: one feels

Turtle dove

that the colour should perhaps relate to the foodplant – say pink for heather feeding, white for bramble etc., but in practice there seems to be no obvious correlation with environmental factors. By early August the young (orange-banded at this stage) fox moth caterpillars (another characteristic heathland/ moorland species) are seen. Grass emerald moths on 19 August. Despite its name this is another heathland species whose larva feeds on gorse. Like most green moths the colour fades quickly in daylight but unlike many of the other emeralds the grass emerald normally rests with hindwings totally covered by its forewings, with the result that after a few days the latter fade to a parchment straw colour whilst the protected hind-wings are still a fine green.

Beautiful brocade moth caterpillars in August on broom, the moths often numerous at night. 'Primrose' plume moths 31 July. These delicate little plume moths are a very pale yellowish white, probably *Leioptilus osteodactylus*. Common darter and brown hawker dragonflies (nearest water must be ½–1 mile away).

Green and gorse shield-bugs, the latter a species of heathland with gorse, sloe-bugs, and bug *Picromeris bidens*, the latter frequently seen with large caterpillar or moth (orange swift on one occasion) impaled on its rostrum (beak).

Birch shield-bug in September, already turning dark brown for winter hibernation (loss of

Green shield-bug

chlorophyll?). Tiny dwarf cream wave moth 19 August, and a comma butterfly.

27 September. Flock of 50 redpolls, a late swift overhead, three linnets (surprisingly few linnets seen on reserve, perhaps areas of gorse are too small). On 29 September a buzzard, a species which is increasing in Bewdley area. Spotted flycatcher on 17 August.

Toads and common lizards both frequent on reserve. Presumably toads must breed in the safari park pools more than half a mile away.

October to December

Male brimstone butterfly at rest on 11 October in a dense broom brush, perhaps preparing for hibernation. Also gorse shield-bugs and shield-bug *Picromeris bidens*. On 1 October a beautiful yellow underwing moth caterpillar – another attractive moth, with wonderfully camouflaged heather-feeding caterpillar.

Flocks of 40–60 redpolls. Redwings on 9 October, sparrowhawks, over 50 fieldfares on 8 November. Also meadow pipits which do not breed on the reserve but are normally present in winter, particularly roosting at night in heather.

On 16 November a ring-tail hen harrier flew across reserve at low level from west to east. The first record as far as I know for the site and the best view I have ever had of this bird.

January and February 1994

First small tortoiseshell on 28 February. Speckled wood butterfly chrysalis. On 12 January a late male winter moth. On 14 January the first male early moth. This is not common on reserve, being a

hawthorn and blackthorn hedge feeder. Full grown fox moth caterpillar found on 19 January under turf: normally hibernating at this time!

Tortrix moth *Acleris notana* flying. This is a small birch-feeding species, appearing in winter in warm and sunny spells, out of hibernation.

Gulls overhead, redpoll flocks, sparrowhawks, mistle thrush singing in January. Fieldfares and redwings often overhead.

Conservation work on the reserve and other events

Mid-July – cutting bracken in Horse-field and Bull-field.

Late July/early August – bracken spraying with Asulox selective herbicide.

September, October and March – scrub, scrub and more scrub

clearance. Digging out small and medium trees and shrubs from heathland, cutting broom in similar situations, coppicing scattered trees and some of woodland edge to recreate height graded hedges. All necessary to conserve open habitats and heather by preventing invasion and take-over by trees.

Litter and removal of burnt out cars – throughout the year. Also repairs to fencing, notices, and clearance of paths.

Fires – can happen almost any time – especially risky from February to May when much vegetation dead and dry (especially bracken), though such fires can be quick and often relatively superficial. Fires often seem beneficial in terms of regrowth afterwards. Perhaps we worry about them too much?

Gorse flowering: western gorse August to October; European gorse mostly March to April, some at other times. Broom flowering late May to June.

Heather: ling in flower at best about 20 August. Bell heather: late June to end September, flowering period more spread out.

Tales from the warden
The stoat

Winter work on the heath can seem boring and might be too lonely for some temperaments on a cold misty February day. On such a day I was eating lunch sitting on the Land Rover, when a rabbit ran along the grassy track towards me. It turned off the track and crouched in the heather. Within seconds a stoat followed, obviously in pursuit, but ran past the crouching rabbit and

disappeared into the heather further along the track. A minute or two later the stoat (or was it a different stoat?) appeared, coming along the track from the original direction. This time it found the rabbit which jumped up, and was immediately leapt upon by the stoat which seized it by the back of the neck. After a brief struggle the rabbit lay still, and the stoat dropped from its neck. Within a few seconds the rabbit exploded into life, and raced off down the track, pursued by the stoat, both eventually disappearing into the heather and out of sight. Later, rabbit squeals from further off suggested that they had become reacquainted.

Stoat

An interesting sequel to this event occurred a little later when a woman, walking a dog, 'rescued' a rabbit which her dog had found, but not injured. The rabbit appeared completely unhurt, but simply crouched in the grass wherever it was placed. I put it near where I was working, where it remained unmoving for at least half an hour, but had gone (presumably under its own steam) by the end of the afternoon.

Exorcism at the Devil's Spittleful
Coming on to the reserve one afternoon from main track, sound of singing and chanting heard through the trees from area of

Devil's Spittleful rock that was more organised than the more normal sounds of kids shouting and playing. On listening from a closer point, the chanting was heard to include "We shall have the power" and to call on Christ's power. Eventually a group of four people were revealed, at which point they were huddled together, one seemingly in prayer, meditation (or severe migraine?). Soon after they quietly departed. Perhaps I witnessed some form of exorcism – I never had the nerve to ask them. Was it because of some incident that had taken place here? Or did they exorcise any place with "Devil" in the name? I wish I had asked, though perhaps the answer might have been boring, and the speculation of not knowing much more interesting.

Duke of York Meadow

A 2 hectare meadow situated next to the Duke of York pub on the south side of the A438 Ledbury to Tewkesbury road in the parish of Berrow. The field lies on Keuper Marl and slopes down gently to a ditch on the northern boundary near the pub. The best time to visit this field is in the spring when the wild daffodils are in flower.

Access is at grid reference SO 782354 on the south side of the main A438 near the Duke of York Inn. The nearest village is Birtsmorton. There is a small car park and picnic area by the road which can be used at any time. The daffodils can be seen well from the car park. The meadow itself is closed from April to August to allow the hay to grow, and again when sheep and cattle are put in to graze the field.

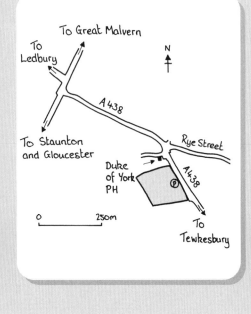

The site is an unimproved lowland meadow which has been designated as an SSSI. Rather low ridge-and-furrow runs down the field to the ditch indicating cultivation in the distant past, although the field has probably been used for hay and pasture for centuries. The field, like Poolhay Meadow reserve (see page 96), was once owned by the nearby Inn. It has never been treated with chemicals and has not been ploughed in recent times. The field is fairly well-drained with neutral or slightly basic soils over rather dry Keuper Marls.

Wild daffodil

The meadow has a rich and beautiful flora with over 120 species of flowering plants recorded. It is an outstanding wild daffodil meadow carpeted with yellow flowers early in spring. There are also cowslips, green-winged orchids, great burnet, pepper-saxifrage, dyer's greenweed and adder's-tongue fern, all typical of old meadows. Bluebells grow under the hedgerows.

To maintain suitable conditions for the flowers the field is farmed. A hay crop grows from April onwards to be cut in July. After the grass has started to grow again cattle or sheep graze the field in autumn and winter.

Butterflies are numerous with over 20 species recorded, including characteristic grassland species such as meadow browns (whose caterpillars feed on a range of grasses) and common blues (whose caterpillars usually prefer bird's-foot-trefoil). In spring and early summer, the large numbers of flowers attract peacock and tortoiseshell butterflies to feed, as well as a variety of bees, flies and other insects.

The wild daffodils present a magnificent sight in early spring and can be enjoyed from the small car park and picnic area. Please do not pick them! It is against the law to do so, but in any case it is much better to leave them for everyone to enjoy, and for them to set seed.

Eades Meadow and Foster's Green Meadows

On 14 May 1954, the doyen of Worcestershire's naturalists Fred Fincher (now in his 90s) found Eades Meadow. It was then part of a small farm in the unspoiled depths of Worcestershire's countryside near Hanbury. He was astonished at the wealth of wild flowers in the field. Forty years on, almost to the day, on 18 May 1994, Fred and an august gathering of eminent persons stood in the field on a cool and windy morning to hear Lord Cranbrook, Chairman of English Nature, declare the site a National Nature Reserve. So great have been the changes in our countryside in the last fifty years that a field full of flowers, once considered commonplace in England, is now a rarity and warrants national recognition.

Because this is farmed land, sensitive to trampling and often grazed by cattle, the field is only open to visitors on special Open Days. Everyone is free to lean on the gate by the road and gaze at the field at any time, but if you would like a closer look, ask the Trust's office for the dates of spring Open Days. Foster's Green Meadows are not open to visitors.

Cowslip

Nowadays Eades Meadow and the adjacent Foster's Green Meadows, which together cover 12½ hectares, are managed as a nature reserve. They lie on heavy clay soils and their interest lies in the large number of plants which grow in the turf and the huge numbers of insects, spiders and other invertebrates they support. Eades Meadow is particularly famous for its meadow saffron in autumn and green-winged orchids in spring, but the colour of the meadow changes daily as different plants come into flower through the spring and summer.

Wild onion

Foster's Green Farm is still farmed. Eades Meadow is grazed by cattle in late autumn and early winter and then left to grow hay. The hay is cut late in the following summer after the flowers have seeded. Following a period of growth the field then is grazed again.

This land has not been ploughed for at least 100 years and has never been treated with chemical fertilisers, herbicides or other agricultural chemicals. Part of the land was once a small orchard and a few apple trees remain. A few large oak trees mark the positions of old field boundaries. The huge elms which once grew in the hedges were killed by Dutch elm disease and their demise opened up the field to the wind and sun. This and several dry summers may have contributed to the decline of meadow saffron in recent years.

diary by Peter Auger

17 April 1993

Cool, bright and changeable. Fairly dry underfoot, with grasses starting to grow well. Main features are cowslips in full bloom and abundant. Marsh-marigolds (kingcups) also in flower. Dark green wild onion patches seem to be spreading.

10 May

Warm and sunny after thundery rain. Plagued by cockchafers. General impression of meadow a mass of purple green-winged orchids and bugle, and yellow cowslips and buttercups with a blue fringe of bluebells. Other features – meadow saffron leaves, adder's-tongue fern, common spotted-orchid leaves, twayblades, and Good Friday grass. Grasses still

short enough to reveal ridge and furrow effect at the top of the meadow. Oak trees at their best with yellow-green leaves. Occasional green-winged orchids and cowslips found in adjacent meadow. Several orange-tip butterflies in vicinity of cuckooflower.

25 June

Warm and sunny, dry underfoot. Tinge of yellow on maturing grasses. Path cut for open day still visible and apparently much used. Common spotted-orchid specimens 45 cm high. Meadow saffron leaves brown and withered. Pepper-saxifrage, saw-wort and common knapweed in flower. Meadow brown butterflies in profusion. Pond line has receded but still well-filled. Much activity from damselflies and dragonflies; no records for the reserve and worth a special survey. Emerged from tour covered in bites from unidentified (and unseen) insects.

13 July

Cloudy, spitting rain, windy, cool. Hay crop ready for mowing, going over and very brown. Horsetail waist high in top corner of meadow. Pond level much reduced, with no sign of dragonflies. Disturbed mallard on water. Sandy brown fungus massed at the foot of the oak trees. Noted St John's-wort and masses of yellow-rattle.

18 August

Hazy sunshine, warm, light breeze. Grass mown three days previously and left in rows to dry. Pond completely dried out and firm enough to walk over bed. Meadow saffron flowers starting to make a display, but obscured by mown hay. A few meadow brown butterflies noted. Brook completely dried up. A forlorn appearance compared with the lushness of May.

14 September

Warmish, sunny – no wind. Meadow saffron still in bloom, after clearance of hay crop. Pond still dried out but base now spongy. Hazel catkins starting to form. Elms regenerating in the southern hedgerow. Noted speckled wood butterfly and jay. Devils'-bit scabious flowering in a few unmown patches around apples trees. Main gate post broken at base.

21 October

Dry sunny – stiff breeze. Gate post temporarily repaired. Very wet

underfoot, with heavy cattle hoof imprints. Herd of 18 cattle concentrated at top end of meadow, and helping in reserve management by grazing the aftermath (the regrowth of grasses after the hay has been cut). Top gate open allowing cattle to move between two meadows at will. Pond full to margins and heavily trampled around the edges. Fruits of the Midland hawthorn very easy to identify in the hedge. Splendid and vivid display of rose hips.

12 November
Sunny, light breeze, mild. Generally wet underfoot with water lying in hollows. Brook running fast and clear. Grey squirrel and several hares noted. Fruits of spindle trees in hedgerow showing bright coral pink in the sunshine, almost like spring blossom. Cattle now removed from meadow, but still much evidence of trampling. Stone coloured fungus which looks like St George's mushroom. New shoots emerging from marsh-marigold plants.

28 December
Heavily overcast, cold. Meadow covered with layer of snow after a very hard frost. No attempt to walk the usual circuit.

14 January 1994
Strong south-west wind, heavy showers, cold. Meadow has water-logged appearance, with brook overflowing, the main pond full and many low-lying areas completely submerged. Flote grass in evidence in pond. Many bluebell bulbs unearthed by moles. Hazel catkins well-developed. A cold, cheerless vista.

11 February
Cold, overcast with a chill wind. Roadside ditch near to overflowing. Gap in hedge allows flock of domestic geese from next farm to graze the grass. Brook rushing along like a mountain stream, very muddy and overflowing in bottom corner near road. General impression – even more waterlogged than in January. Style broken near plank bridge across brook. Signs of spring – emerging dog's mercury and lords-and-ladies leaves.

12 March
Cold, damp. Still very waterlogged, with occasional patches of standing water. Little sign of growth in meadow or hedgerow. Pair of hares exhibiting courtship behaviour. Hazel catkins in abundance.

Feckenham Wylde Moor

The 11½ hectares of Feckenham Wylde Moor reserve are the last remnants of an extensive marsh which once lay in the valley of the Brandon Brook, south of Feckenham. The land was drained in around 1850 and turned to agriculture. In more recent times the drainage system became blocked and wetland was restored. The Trust bought the area and established the reserve in 1981, excavating the large pool the following year. The reserve is underlaid by base-rich clays of the Keuper Marl and much of it is covered by a surface layer of fen-peat, an uncommon soil type in Worcestershire.

Access is via Moors Lane which runs south from the village of Feckenham. This track is unsuitable for cars and there is no parking space on the reserve. Visitors should park in the Feckenham village public car park and walk to the reserve. Moors Lane joins the main road in Feckenham at grid reference SP 011613. Walk to the far end of the reserve where there is a bird-watching hide overlooking the small pool. From there a marked path leads visitors round the reserve. Please do not leave the trail as there are unexpected boggy areas and deep wells and channels.

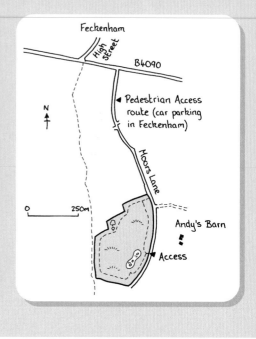

by Mike Bretherton

January 1993

The usual work party, always held on the third Sunday in the month, attracted ten volunteers who worked in total 43.5 man-hours, a record to date.

February

A mute swan has joined four Canada geese on the pool. Snipe in meadows.

A great day on the 18th! A badger has taken up residence in the bank at the far end of the pool, leaving unmistakable signs by way of bedding outside the sett and a freshly used latrine. There has always been a well-used track along the reserve western boundary, complete with a tree trunk regularly used for sharpening badger claws, but this is the first record of a badger resident. Somewhat surprising as nowhere except the bank by the pool is more than a few centimetres above the winter water table.

The log in the hide records six snipe seen in Home Ground, and the usual wrens in the willows by the hide. The swan is still with us, with an orange ring (number 28N) on its left leg. Weather unseasonably mild.

Another good work party on the 21st, working on pollarding willows and path-making on a mild and sunny day. Rewarded by sighting a woodcock and snipe in Hill Piece,

Snipe

with numerous redwings and fieldfares.

March

Signs of spring! Seven Canada geese disputing territory, with one pair nesting on the far island. Three male and two female tufted duck, several reed buntings, a fox hunting in the reedbed. Eight snipe at various places round the reserve. Cock pheasants. Badger still using pool sett, but the swan has departed.

On the 11th, a lone greylag goose is with the Canada geese on the pool. Five snipe in Home Ground, flock of redwings in the alders. Colt's-foot in full flower in front of the hide. Kestrel hunting over the reserve and perched on a fence post.

Possible disaster! Our grazier of several years' standing confirms that he is giving up because of ill health, The four Hereford cattle which were such an attractive sight in our meadows last year have been sold. How will we provide the grazing needed to maintain the diversity of plant species which led to the Wylde Moor being declared an SSSI?

Our annual mass spawning of toads is now in full swing round the edge of the pool, particularly just in front of the hide. The number of pairs really is impressive, and must represent a population explosion made possible following the excavation of the pool by the Trust in 1981. The heron now visits daily to take advantage of this easy feast, and no doubt toad numbers will decline to a less spectacular level eventually as a result.

Reed bunting

April

A Canada goose sitting on a nest on the first island. One little grebe present – will he/she find a mate and give us our first breeding record? A hare in Middle Ley Close, cowslips just flowering in Home Ground.

This month's work party concentrated on burning off the enormous quantity of brushwood left after the pollarding of the willows alongside Moors Lane in March. We do not want a forest of willows springing up wherever a fallen twig has taken root on the wet ground! Without qualified chainsaw operators we can do nothing with the logs, some of which are nearly a metre in diameter. We have arranged for a local person to cut them up and take them away free of charge in exchange for his labour. A reminder, that we should find a place on a Trust chainsaw course for one of our

younger work party volunteers – firewood from the reserve is an asset we need to exploit.

The cowslips are in full flower in Home Ground, the meadow at the south end of the reserve. A count shows that numbers have increased slightly since the year before; there is now also an attractive colony conveniently placed close to the new route of the reserve path for showing off to visitors. Male reed buntings are now everywhere, perched high on the reed heads to establish their territories for the nesting season. A welcome contrast to winter, when the reedbed often appears empty.

May

One of the many happenings in Worcestershire Wildlife Week is a guided walk through the reserve. This has become an annual event, and is particularly welcomed by the Reserve Management Committee because many thousands of Wildlife Week leaflets are distributed reaching many people who have never even heard of a Nature Reserve at Feckenham, let alone visited it. The fresh interest and enthusiasm such visitors bring with them is both stimulating and enjoyable.

The walk starts from the car park in the village. On this occasion 28 people came, and despite a heavy shower of rain towards the end we collected £22 in the badger box. One year we were somewhat startled to see a marsh harrier overhead as we walked round, our first record at Feckenham. Unfortunately the Christopher Cadbury reserve manager (that is,

Ragged-Robin

me!), who was in front with another party, failed to look up at the right moment; one would have thought some instinct or divine guidance looked after a visiting expert from the Trust's premier bird reserve on such occasions!

On 15 May a grass snake sunning itself in the second meadow did not wait to be photographed, but fortunately our resident photographer, Gordon Forrest, has many slides of snakes on the reserve, where grass snakes are common. They probably account for the relative scarcity of frogs. Cuckooflower is a typical plant of wet meadows, foodplant of the orange-tip butterfly, and today in full flower everywhere. The cowslips are over, but ragged-Robin is just beginning to give a pink tinge to the meadows.

June

Reserve Open Day. In preparation, a path has been cut through the northern meadows, passing the best of the ragged-Robin and the colony of common spotted-orchids on the way. The Trust landrover provided a ferry service from the village car park, and two stalls provided hot and cold drinks and cover for Trust display boards. About 40 people came. Though we were not able to match a previous occasion, when a guided party at the Open Day seated in the hide was treated to a flying display by a hobby taking dragonflies over the pool, we did see the first banded demoiselles of the year on the main pool. These probably come in from the Brandon brook nearby, as the larvae prefer running water.

July

There are 16 species of dragonflies and damselflies recorded at Feckenham Wylde Moor, making this one of the best sites in the county to see them, helped by an identification chart on display in the hide. The first to appear each year is the large red damselfly in April, and by July all the others should have made an appearance. On a sunny day the emperor dragonfly, four-spotted chaser and brown hawker can all be seen hunting over the pool. The sight of they themselves being hunted by a hobby is a rare occurrence, but for the patient watcher there is always a chance.

The meadows are being mown by a contractor, and if the weather and our finances permit, the hay will be baled and carried away.

This operation, followed by grazing in the autumn, is essential if the full range of wild flowers and grasses are to be maintained. Strangely enough a relatively impoverished soil is better than one rich in nutrients and particularly nitrogen. Fertiliser and even an accumulation of rotting vegetation encourages a few species of grass at the expense of everything else.

A neighbouring farmer has now agreed to graze his bullocks on the reserve this autumn, which is a great relief. Current conditions in agriculture are such that it is sometimes impossible to find graziers for 'unimproved' (no artificial fertiliser) grassland.

For the first time little grebes have bred successfully, very conveniently nesting on the island closest to the hide and in full view. Somehow the pool has recently acquired a fish population to join the great crested newts and other amphibians we have always had, and the little grebe can sometimes be seen with a fish in its beak.

August

This being a wetland, much of the reserve path is inevitably very muddy, the water table being at or above ground level throughout the winter in the sedge and reed area. Here our monthly work party has been building a raised path with brushwood and logs cut from the alder coppice, capped with peat obtained by digging small pools nearby.

One advantage of this regular clearance along the strip of raised ground represented by the path is a

much increased frequency of some of the more colourful wetland plants such as water figwort and purple-loosestrife, now freed from complete dominance by sedges and reed. Occasionally the walker may encounter the local fox, disturbed from sleep on a sheltered tussock in the reedbed. By the dragonfly pools one can attract the emperor and broad-bodied chaser dragonflies to settle and be photographed by placing a light-coloured stick at the water's edge.

October

Now we are well into autumn, and the work party is using the brushcutter to cut back the rushes and sedges on the west side of the main pool and on the two islands, hoping to encourage winter visiting ducks such as teal and pochard.

One of our number possesses a home-made coracle, which must be the most unstable boat ever invented, and the Reserve Manager's attempt to cross to one of the islands lasted less than thirty seconds. Fortunately, for once, no photographs were taken to record this humiliation.

November

We have decided to try our hand at laying 30 metres of hawthorn hedge alongside Moors Lane, planted 15 years ago when a gas pipeline was laid across the reserve, and therefore young enough to stand the best chance of recovering from our amateur activities. 'Before and after' photographs are being taken to bear witness to our success or otherwise. We are off to a good start, but it is already clear that even the short stretch we have chosen to tackle this year will need several days work.

December

Planting trees on a cold winter's day requires encouragement and reward for the workers, provided this year in the form of a fierce bonfire as we burn off the hedge cuttings, round which we break for lunch and to entertain visitors invited to see us at work with pigs in blankets (sausages in baked potatoes) and hot soup.

We are planting several more tree species amongst the ash and field maple planted the year after purchase of the reserve and now well-established. Rowan and wild crab apple, with alder in the wettest spot, will provide food for birds and add a touch of colour.

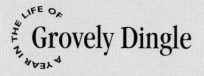

Grovely Dingle

Grovely Dingle is a deep valley cut into a hillside south-east of Longbridge on the outskirts of Birmingham. Several converging streams have cut deep ravines which drain into a central steam and a small pool at the southern end of the ravine. The valleys are mainly wooded with oak and ash. There are many woodland flowers, and the damp valleys are good for ferns and mosses. There are several patches of old meadow land.

Access is restricted. A permit must first be sought from the Trust's office.

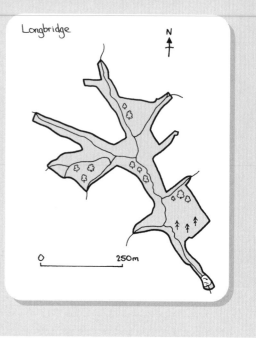

by Eric Hawkeswood

January–March 1993

The green-clad pines in the wood near the reserve entrance were a cheering welcome for our January work party for a day clearing encroaching hawthorn scrub from one of the two ancient meadows. We worked in glorious sunshine with a magical hoar frost covering the trees.

Walking through the steep dingles I put up three different woodcock, a rare surprise! Then a pheasant that waited to go up until I had almost trodden on it – a surprise not so good for the heart!

April–June

April is a real month of change in the Dingle. The fresh greens of the new hawthorn leaves colour the hedgerows, and as the month progressed blackcaps and willow warbler arrived and the bluebells started to put on a show: to quote one visitor "the oakwood looks like it's got a blue shag-pile carpet!"

May is the best time of year! The Dingle is covered with the colours of bluebells, yellow archangel, wood-sorrel and greater stitchwort, complemented by splashes of red campion and yellow goldilocks buttercup in damp shady areas.

Mistle thrush

July–September

Our major speciality, wood barley, has done well this year, we have found it in three different areas now, a success story for a county rarity.

In September the reserve resounded to the noise of brush-cutter and mowers as the meadows were cut for hay. We have done this for three years now and removed the cuttings. The diversity of meadow plants is certainly increasing.

October–December

On every walk at this time I put up what seemed to be hundreds of wood pigeons roosting in the pines, and once at least twenty pheasants went up, shattering the calm.

The year has gone full circle. One impression has remained clearly in my mind: a mistle thrush singing loudly from the top of an ash tree. Despite the strong wind and rain it was living up to its alternative name of storm-cock. A sign that although hardship lay ahead, the Dingle is ready for another cycle of life!

Hornhill Wood

A 5½ hectare wood managed by the Trust under agreement with the owner. Over the last 20 years the Trust has revived full coppice-with-standards management, as used in most lowland woods for hundreds of years until it declined this century when demand for underwood (firewood, faggots, stakes, wattle) disappeared. Classical coppice-with-standards consists of hazel thickets (coppice) growing beneath big oak trees (standards). The coppice is cut every 7–20 years in blocks. The big trees are cut for timber, ensuring that new standards are grown to replace those felled. This entire cycle of the woodland resource is also very good for a wide range of wildlife. The cyclical activity constantly recreates a series of habitat conditions used by different species at different stages of the cycle; in effect a man-made speeded-up version of natural events.

The Trust does not own Hornhill Wood and there are restrictions on access. Please contact the Trust's office before visiting the wood. Note: nearby Hill Wood is not now a Trust reserve, and should not be visited.

Great tit

by Tom Haynes

April 1993

The sweet song of the willow warbler ripples through the wood. A whole wave of them has arrived from Africa. Do they travel in close convoy (the Hornhill contingent) or drop individually out of a huge armada passing over the county throughout the night? No matter, they're back – joining their close cousins the chiffchaffs and more distant relatives the blackcaps in enriching the bird song chorus.

Herb-Paris

This is the month when the benefits of all those back-breaking hours of work throughout the winter begin to reveal themselves and gladden the volunteers' hearts (or is it just the end of the main work party season which is so welcome?). The wood looks fresh and colourful and every visit can turn up something different – the reappearance of an old favourite perhaps, or a first sighting for the reserve. The species lists for birds (about 80) and plants (about 200) are still growing annually, if only slowly, whilst most other floral and faunal groups are very under-recorded.

The recently coppiced plots are bright with primroses and violets, and with early bluebells later in the month. Along the narrow paths and broader rides these flowers are joined by emerging leaves and flower spikes of many common spotted-orchids and a few greater butterfly-orchids. Early-purple orchids are not regular. Here and there are patches of herb-Paris, a species indicative of ancient woodland but attractive too in its own quiet undemonstrative way.

Resident birds are now well into their breeding season whilst most summer migrants are just arriving. The wood resounds with song as they establish territories and strive to attract a mate. Blackcap and garden warbler, cuckoo and the tardy spotted flycatcher are all regular whilst wood warbler, nightingale and pied flycatcher have bred occasionally and may do so again any year.

Around the nest boxes the blue and great tits are ferrying moss and

feathers as their nest building reaches its peak. Putting up these artificial nest sites compensates for the lack of dead and dying trees which would naturally provide nest holes. The majority of our 30 tit boxes are occupied every year and the fledging rate is very high. Other boxes provided for different species have been less successful but jackdaws are busy around the largest boxes high up in the oaks.

May

"Can I carry the ladder?", "Can we go down that way?", "Can I carry the ladder?", "Are there any foxes in here?" (nervously), "Where's our nest box?" " Can I carry ...?"

This is a favourite month for visitors and none are more welcome than the young children who come to see their nest boxes. All our tit boxes and a few of the others are leased out, mostly to or for children, and they are invited to make a visit during the nesting season when they will see activity at some boxes and may be shown the contents of their own. The warden will also try to find other things to interest them such as creepy crawlies under a log, frogs in the pond, or maybe the remains of a sparrowhawk's kill. Sometimes they are excited just to be in the wood, to experience the scary thrill of wandering down a narrow path on their own not knowing that it will bring them back safely onto the

Spotted flycatcher

ride. Some get the biggest kick out of carrying the warden's ladder.

Showing any appreciative visitors around 'our' reserve gives most wardens great satisfaction. It is an opportunity to air one's knowledge (limited though that may be), to show how much work has been done and to demonstrate the beneficial effects of it. Above all it is a time to enjoy the wood and to share that enjoyment with others.

In early May the last of the summer migrant birds return: spotted flycatchers announce their presence with penetrating squeaks like an un-oiled wheelbarrow, whilst the turtle dove purrs its

soporific song. Unfortunately the turtle dove is quite scarce in this part of the county and we cannot rely on having them in the wood every year.

This is the month for that masochistic activity "The Dawn Chorus": forcing oneself out of a warm bed in order to listen to the birds! It may perhaps be dry and still but it is invariably cold, at least to begin with. In recent years Worcestershire Wildlife Week dawn chorus events have given many people a chance to experience the magic and wonder of up to 50 species singing within the space of about two hours in just a few acres of wood and farmland. And what a feeling of superiority over lesser mortals who did not make the effort, and how good breakfast tastes when one returns home!

This year the herb-Paris is as good as ever with one patch over 100 plants strong. As their pale flower spikes wither the orchids are reaching their prime. Walking the path along the western edge of the wood I look for a large white bluebell, because nearby is another of our regulars, the best greater butterfly-orchid spike. Though tall and showy this flower can be surprisingly difficult to find unless one knows just where to look, and this is where the bluebell comes in: it is a whiter shade of pale and easier to spot under the trees.

June

The hum of innumerable insects provides a constant backdrop. The remnants of birdsong enliven the quietness of the wood. The rich variety and volume of spring is already largely just a memory. One species after another falls silent as the need to proclaim presence is replaced by the rigours of breeding. A chiffchaff's penetrating song contrasts with the cooing of wood pigeons and the contact notes of a family party of tits from one of our 'rent-a-nest' boxes. Suddenly a tremendous racket breaks out as a tawny owl is discovered at his roost by a couple of blackbirds, backed up by a robin and several wrens.

Colour also is less varied this month, not counting the many shades of green of course! Unlike the showy massed ranks of spring flowers, those of early summer are, with one exception, small and thinly scattered, but several of them have other characteristics: figwort, herb-Robert and hedge woundwort all smell when bruised, the latter disgustingly so! The exception is the common spotted-orchid for which this is another good year. The south ride has hundreds of them, many up to two feet tall. Just a few years back we had a mere handful near the top of this ride but now they are everywhere. The wild strawberries add the chance of indulging another of the senses for anyone patient enough to pick a few of these tiny fruits before the voles get them!

A white admiral zooms up and down the edges of the ride where garlands of fragrant honeysuckle festoon the hazel. The spell of fine weather at the month's end has hastened the emergence of several butterfly species, and ringlets, meadow browns and large skippers perch on the grasses in the sunny rides. Two or three damselfly and dragonfly species await positive identification. Presumably they come from one of our tiny pools, which contain comparatively clean water despite the thick layer of pondweed now covering the water surfaces.

This is often the time when we will visit the nearby Hill Wood. Formerly hazel coppice with oak standards just like Hornhill, it has not been managed for over 20 years. Twice the size of Hornhill, and relatively undisturbed, it has a wild unkempt appearance and might be expected to have a richer wildlife, but surveys have proved that fauna and flora have been adversely affected by the denser shade and comparative lack of habitat variety. In 1986 a Common Birds Census

showed Hornhill to have 33% more species and 50% more pairs of breeding birds than its big sister. This is both the proof and the justification for all our work in maintaining the coppice cycle in Hornhill Wood.

July

Bird-wise this can be a dull month but there is always hope in a birdwatcher's heart. Hope was amply rewarded some years ago by one of my most memorable sightings in the reserve. Taking part in the botanical survey, I was giving my back a rest (do botanists all have chronic back ache?) when a movement caught my eye and there right above us was a female goshawk being escorted out of the area by the local pair of kestrels, which appeared merlin-sized beside the huge hawk. It passed straight over and I have never seen one here since, though I am ever hopeful.

The botanical survey is the longest running survey in Hornhill and measures both the rate of re-growth of the coppiced hazel and the rise and fall of other flora after the plot is coppiced. For about four years the density and variety of species increases annually before the regrowing bramble and hazel begin to shade them out. After ten years, when the plot is due to be coppiced again, there are very few species thriving beneath the dense shade, though most plant species are merely lying dormant in the

Goshawk

ground biding their time until we let in the sunlight again.

Summer, of course, is not a dull time so far as butterflies are concerned and around the tops of the tallest oaks flit purple hairstreaks – one of my favourite species but not easy to see well unless you are very lucky and find one nectaring on a low bramble for a change. Gatekeepers (or hedge browns) commonly first appear now: the bramble beside the path from the gate to the first ride being a favourite area for them and meadow browns.

Violet helleborine

August

Agrimony, betony, centaury, devils'-bit scabious – it looks like a botanist's dictionary, but these all flower in August continuing the seasons of colour on the rides.

Many species need the open, sunny rides to thrive, but there is one very notable exception to this generalisation and this year provided a remarkable record. The violet helleborine is one of our rarer plants which has been found in Hornhill on only a few occasions (just five to my personal knowledge) and in numbers ranging from one to about six plants. In the last two years a few were found in one area and we have impatiently awaited their appearance again this year. We must have missed them in July because this month there they were again in the same spot, 30–45 cm tall in full flower. As the work party moved on, however, more and more were spotted until everyone downed tools and made a thorough search of the woodland edge. Well inside the thickets in dense shade where almost nothing else can survive, clump after clump of helleborines was found until the almost unbelievable total of 75 was reached!

September

As the work party moves along a path, a slight movement just off to one side catches an eye. Ever glad of a diversion we all gather round to inspect the remains of a wasps' nest. A badger was here last night, or more likely earlier this morning, digging out the nest for the adults and their grubs and the few survivors are still crawling into cover. Paw prints in the moist soil confirm the raider's identity, but not many other predators would tackle such a dangerous job anyway. There is no badgers' sett in the wood but evidence of their visits are occasionally found – this is not the first plundered wasp nest I have seen.

September is the traditional month for starting work on a new coppice plot. We start by slashing out the bramble, both dead and alive, so that we can more easily get at the hazel stools to cut them down. Any desirable shrubs or young trees which look particularly vulnerable are marked with string to reduce the risk of their inadvertent removal by over-eager workers and then the main task of coppicing can begin. Our hazel is mostly in very good health because, like a garden rose, it responds to regular hard 'pruning' and grows back more vigorously than ever,

Badger

throwing out more young shoots in an ever expanding circle. The coppice stumps or 'stools' can be very old; given regular coppicing the root stock can live for centuries.

October

The month of the jay – this might be a suitable description for October, at least for me. Rarely the most conspicuous of birds, jays are far more often heard than seen. Their raucous cries like tearing linen ring through the woods but they are justifiably wary of man. Persecution by several generations of gamekeepers has ensured that, but they are also one of the most attractive of species and this is the time to see them. Suddenly they appear almost everywhere as they feast on the acorn crop, taking many away to bury in the leaf litter on the woodland floor. Large single oaks in the surrounding fields and hedgerows are often centres of attraction with a constant to-ing and fro-ing between trees and wood. A buried acorn may be recovered by the bird later when other food is hard to find, but occasionally one may germinate and grow into a fine big oak.

Jay

November

The stillness of the wood is broken only by the constant dripping of moisture. Suddenly the harsh call of a cock pheasant rings through the trees and the observant visitor may see many of them, especially under

the cover of the hazel or scuttling across a ride. More leisurely views can be had at the seed dispensers which the gamekeepers provide for them at two or three locations. One or two cocks with an indeterminate number of hen birds often survive the winter slaughter to breed around the wood edge but the vast majority of birds seen will have been 'artificially' reared and released in one of the other woods nearby to provide the main quarry of the shooting syndicate which visits all the local woods.

The idealistic or purist conservationist will no doubt object strongly to this practice, especially on a nature reserve, but the more pragmatic realise that were it not for this commercial activity then these woods would not survive beyond the present day because they provide little if any other income to their owners. A shooting ban would therefore result in the loss of more wildlife than just the pheasants, but in any case we have no choice at Hornhill but to accept it as a fact of life (the Trust does not own Hornhill Wood but manages it under an Agreement with the owner).

December

Not all this year's fruits have disappeared yet, a few rose hips and hawthorn berries have escaped the thrushes but the large old guelder-rose near the southern edge of the wood is still laden with waxy bright red berries. Meanwhile the honeysuckle is already in bud again and the hazels are also beginning to develop their

catkins though the small female flowers will not appear before the spring.

Somewhere a nuthatch calls just once and then falls silent again. Even in the spring this small acrobat is often overlooked amongst the oaks; Hornhill's nuthatches are remarkably quiet. We have never seen more than one pair so presumably they do not need to defend territories and the need and stimulus for demonstrative song are largely lacking. Whether or not this is an adequate explanation I cannot say but it is undeniably the case that, whilst in other woods the nuthatch can be extremely noisy with a wide range of penetrating calls and whistles, we hear them rarely even though breeding has been proved on several occasions when they conveniently used tit nest boxes.

January 1994

Snow blankets the ground and even trees and shrubs retain a covering unless the wind shakes it down. Sound is muffled and this familiar and much loved little wood looks strangely alien and threatening in its bleakness. Birds and animals are now really up against it having to spend much of their waking hours searching for food to bolster them against the bitter cold and piercing winds, and many will not awake the following morning unless they can replace the loss during the previous night of up to one third of their bodyweight. Suddenly, clichéd phrases like 'survival of the fittest' and 'nature red in tooth and claw' come to mind as the white carpet reveals evidence which otherwise would go unnoticed. A scattering of feathers and the bloody remains of

a goldfinch's head reveals that a sparrowhawk has made an early kill amongst the thistles along a nearby hedgerow and brought it into the wood for consumption. Stoats are rarely seen but their tracks show that our rabbits or voles have lured them in for a hunt, though on this occasion there is no sign of a kill.

February

This year February heralds a major burst of activity on the work party front as various groups attempt to coppice most of the ½ hectare plot before the advancing breeding season brings work to a halt again. Great clouds of smoke are sometimes to be seen as bonfires are started to burn up the hazel, other shrubs and brambles. There is, of course, an environmentally un-friendly aspect to this practice

which is quite at odds with my dislike of stubble burning and all other forms of pollution. Unfortunately it is the only way to get rid of most of the cut material for which there is only a small demand.

Primroses are beginning to show now but there is little other colour as yet. The hazel catkins are adding their dangling contributions – though somewhat pale individually there are a lot of them! "Whatever happens to all the hazelnuts?" visitors ask, to which I reply "ask the grey squirrels"! They eat all of the nuts before they are even ripe.

Violets may also begin to appear this month but a more conspicuous plant is lords-and-ladies whose blunt arrow shaped leaves burst out of the ground all over the place. Known also as

cuckoopint, parson-in-the-pulpit and Adam and Eve, this flower has a disgusting smell which attracts small flies which then become trapped until guard hairs within the sheath protecting the fleshy stem wither, by which time they have completed their task of pollination, or carry pollen with them to the next plant.

March

March is the month which, more than any other, can be regarded as the turn of the woodland manager's year. There is often a somewhat frantic scramble to complete the winter's work programme before the advancing bird breeding season forces us, in their interests, to stop. In addition, the pace of change and growth in the wood quickens and more and more we want to take

time out and just enjoy it all, waiting impatiently for the return of our favourite species and to see the results of all our work.

We look back on another busy year during which we have successfully continued the centuries old tradition of woodland coppicing. In the process we have maintained or improved this little patch of our county for a range of wildlife, nothing very spectacular we would be the first to admit, but a pleasing variety nevertheless in a wood which has a pleasant and friendly feel to it for most of its visitors. If our management agreement is renewed for a further period this year then why not join that lucky band of people and sample the delights of Hornhill Wood either as a visitor or as a work party diehard?

Hunthouse Wood

Hunthouse and Winricks Woods (about half of Dumbleton Dingle SSSI) are just south of Mamble on the north side of the Teme valley. The reserve is a steep-sided valley with several side streams cutting deeply down into the Carboniferous coal measures. Outcrops of limestones, sandstones and occasionally coal can be seen: part of the dingle was once Hunthouse colliery. Part of this reserve is one of the most impenetrable and undisturbed woods in the county with a rich and varied wildlife. The site has been managed by the Trust since 1976.

The reserve is open at all times to members carrying membership cards. Access is from the Clows Top to Frith Common Road at SO 701706 where a private road leads to the old Hunthouse Colliery and M&M Timber Company. Please do not park on the track or block the entrance in any way as the track is in constant use by lorries. Do not drive down the track: you may be locked in or your car damaged by large timber lorries. Park on nearby roadside verges or on the layby near Foxley Farm and walk down the track to the wood. The reserve entrance is about ¼ mile on the right. A circular route runs through the wood. Please follow it closely as steep slopes and small cliffs by the stream are dangerous.

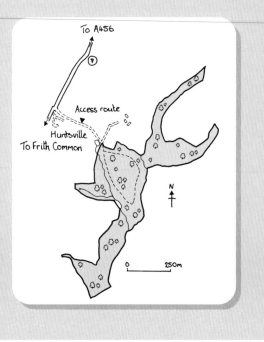

by Andrew Santer

Winter

The turn of the year brings a new feel to the wood, one of optimism, almost a sensing of all that sap ready to rise, and all those shoots waiting to push through the leaf litter.

There is great beauty in the woods, especially on clear, rain-washed days when westerly winds rattle the tree tops, black against a backdrop of brilliant blue or the towering galleons of cumulus, and low sunlight illuminates the silver birches to dazzling intensity. Or after heavy snowfall, so rare these last few years, when dark trees in a landscape of white set-off small details to great effect: a bunch of orange-yellow catkins, or the first green leaves of dangling honeysuckle tendrils.

Small-leaved lime

The woods are mostly silent except in late afternoons when the blackbird roosting alarm calls are joined by the calls of tawny and little owls. Occasionally the eerie cries of foxes or the barking of muntjac deer can be heard.

The smaller resident birds tend now to form one or two large flocks of mixed species, loosely organised and constantly flitting about the canopy. If one of these groups surrounds you, then glimpses of blue, great, long-tailed, coal and marsh tits, goldcrest, treecreeper, nuthatch and great spotted woodpecker are likely to be your reward.

All three species of woodpecker are found on the reserve, but although the green can often be heard, it is the great spotted that is most likely to be seen. When following the main path around the reserve, look at the lime trees by the wooden bridge for signs of these birds seeking the sugary sap. The bark is pock-marked by many lines of small holes made by woodpeckers.

Most management work at this time of year involves scrub clearance and coppicing a system of glades. In many ways the most difficult work on any reserve is the initial capital work, the felling and clearing of dense scrub and well-developed woodland in the case of Hunthouse Wood. Work has been proceeding on this major project for five years and would have been impossible without the hard work and dedication of the volunteers from the Stourbridge and Wyre Forest Local Groups.

For the toughest jobs, and there are plenty, there are regular visits by the Worcestershire Conservation Volunteers, a group whose skills and professionalism are outstanding.

The stimulus for this work comes from the need to safeguard and extend the habitats of most of the reserve's 24 recorded species of butterfly, in conjunction with the opening up of suitable habitat on the eastern side of the reserve. This is the 3½ hectares of old, rough pasture known as Tunnerton's Rough, a south facing bank not quite "tumbled down to woodland" but grown either into dense scrub or glades dominated by rampant bracken.

In late winter, when the ground flora of disturbed sites is at its lowest ebb, is the time when the reserves coal mining past is most easily traced. Shafts were sunk and adits driven to win the Five Foot or Main Coal, here six feet thick and of quite good quality, and outcropping or lying at shallow depths in the valley bottoms. To carry the coal out of the wood a whole series of tramways, inclines, sidings, engine sites and tips were constructed, most of these visible today only to the experienced eye among the trees and shrubbery. The main circular path follows the line of the most important tramway for part of its

length passing through the grassed-over tips of Bayton No. 3 Colliery.

The last coal was mined here in 1947, but mining continued at the adjacent Hunthouse No. 10 Colliery until flooding caused its closure in 1973. The site of Worcestershire's last mine is now occupied by M&M Timber. It is also worth remembering that rural unemployment is a serious concern (the mine's closure led to the loss of about 45 jobs) and businesses such as M&M fulfil a vital role in the economy of the countryside. They also provide an opportunity for greater awareness and understanding on both sides of what are sometimes conflicting arguments. The manager of M&M, Mr M. Harding, takes a great interest in the woods and their proximity to the site ensures a useful degree of monitoring of what goes on when wardens can't be there.

Spring

April is one of the best months to visit the reserve and for the reserve manager provides a welcome break between the demands of winter's felling and clearing and the mowing and bracken control of summer. Sunny weather brings patches of the beautiful wood anemone into flower and, on damper ground, the odorous ramsons, while bugle, violets and wild strawberry dot and star the grassy areas. For a regrettably short while the magnificent crab apples glow a breath-taking pink in bright

Buzzard

Wild strawberry

sunshine as they blossom on Tunnerton's Rough.

By the end of the month migrants have returned from warmer lands to join the resident birds, filling the woods with song and movement. Overhead, the mewing of buzzards is a regular accompaniment on many sunny days and sooner or later their distinctive shape will be seen as they soar and circle above the woods and surrounding meadows. Occasionally they may be spotted indulging in what can only be described as an activity of sheer exhilaration: a pair of birds circling higher and higher until they become tiny dots then, one at a time, folding their wings to drop like a stone through the air, only opening the wings again to go into a shallow curved flight a short distance above the treetops.

The spring flowers continue to delight throughout May, especially bugle, found in patches all over the reserve. Throughout the month butterflies can be seen on the wing including brimstone, peacock, comma, and small tortoiseshells emerging from hibernation, along with holly blue, speckled wood and orange-tip. On the grassed-over coal-tips the dingy skipper darts up and down its territory; with its small size and dull coloration it is easy to overlook.

Later the beautiful pearl-bordered fritillary may be seen flying in search of its food plant: violets growing in the right situation. This species is rarely recorded, though whether this is due to its scarcity or simply lack of

observers at the right time is hard to tell.

Summer

In the first week of June common spotted-orchids are flowering in the grassy glades along the main path. Growing on old coal waste the colony contains, in a good year, up to two hundred flower spikes. Other distinctive species growing here include eyebright, heath speedwell, tufted vetch and dyer's greenweed.

Silver-washed fritillary

May and June bring out a particular nuisance at Hunthouse Wood: bracken. Bracken fulfils a couple of useful functions, it provides dense cover for small birds and mammals and their nests, and shades the ground flora during hot, dry spells. However, it is very invasive and after a while kills off the ground flora leaving a thick accumulation of litter. It is also poisonous and the spores are thought to be carcinogenic if inhaled; later in the season face masks are a must when mowing.

Left to its own devices bracken would smother the paths and ground flora, thus eliminating food and nectar plants for butterflies and invertebrates.

Research suggests that a bracken plant has up to 70 active buds and a couple of hundred dormant ones per square metre. Experience suggests that cutting bracken activates dormant buds and so, despite regular cutting, bracken will continue to appear densely and regularly for several years. To see it appear year after year despite constant attention is rather worrying, but in the end it will die off.

Mid-summer does have its consolation of course, especially the sight of a silver-washed fritillary, gliding in and out of sunlit glades in search of violets and a suitable nearby tree trunk on which to lay its eggs. Numbers of this butterfly have increased due to sensitive management and this year four were observed on one thistle head alone.

Autumn

Squirrels, seemingly absent through the spring and summer are suddenly everywhere over the hazel branches. Unseen, but active, are

the dormice, no doubt beginning the task of assembling winter nests. We have no idea of numbers of these secretive mammals having only ever seen two, but parts of the reserve have abundant hazel, honeysuckle and dense cover, ideal for dormice and left untouched by any management work.

Around this time birdsong begins again, the most noticeable being the rather monotonous 'seep seep' song of the bullfinch, while out on Tunnerton's Rough goldfinches flit between branches and thistle seed heads just like the Edward Thomas poem "The Hollow Wood":

Wild service-tree

Out in the sun the goldfinch flits
Along the thistle-tops, flits and twists
Above the hollow wood
Where birds swim like fish.

Gradually the leaves turn and fall, filling otherwise silent days with a steady rattle and patter. The localised wild service-tree, with its beautiful autumn shades, is only found in isolated pockets away from visitors, so pride of place goes to the field maple whose delicate leaves turn bright yellow in October sunshine.

Winter again

After October comes my least favourite time of year, in or out of the woods: the sombre, gloom-gathering wet or misty short days when a mask of dullness seems to slip over the damp dark trunks and rotting leaves and solace is sought in the glow and warmth of a bonfire. But, even so, there are still magical rewards. Roger and I were clearing scrub on Tunnerton's Rough in mid-December, a dull, damp day, when, without warning in the gathering gloom of late afternoon, the cloud lifted and a beam of sunlight broke through a gap. It bathed us and the woodland around us, for just two amazing minutes, in a most awe-inspiring light of green with a touch of gold. Then snap, out, as if by a switch. But, then, that is the magic of Hunthouse Wood: around each corner a contrast of habitat, some interesting flora or fauna or a magical interplay between light and texture to interest and delight.

Ipsley Alders Marsh

This 18 hectare site was designated a nature reserve in 1967 by the Redditch Development Corporation. After many years of involvement in the management of the area the Trust purchased the site in 1985. Ipsley Alders is a fen marsh, a rare habitat in the Midlands, with up to 1.5 metres of sedge peat overlying blue-green clay. It is well supplied with spring water rising beneath the peat and producing waterlogged conditions over much of the site. It is managed as a grazed marsh with a small number of cattle on the site for much of the year to maintain structural variation within the grassland and marsh.

The reserve is open at all times. Cattle graze on the reserve so please shut gates and keep dogs on a lead. Ipsley Alders is about 2 miles east of Redditch town centre at Winyates Green. Access is off Alders Drive opposite the entrance to Whitehouse Lane at grid reference SP 076677. Park on the road verge or on nearby roads. There is also an entrance near the Winyates Green meeting rooms on opposite side of the marsh. The marsh is dangerously boggy in places and you are advised to wear wellingtons, to take care, and to follow paths.

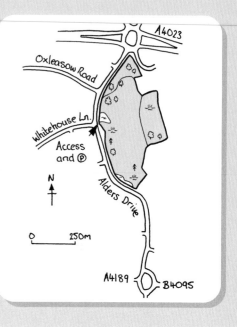

by Tony Jackson

January 1993

The marsh itself looks rather dull, but flocks of tits move through the bordering woods, boosted by numerous birds which make a living feeding at bird tables in the surrounding housing estates.

On a walk across the marsh you are likely to disturb snipe. Common snipe leap into the air and fly off into the distance, but for every twelve common snipe you are likely to disturb one smaller Jack snipe. Jacks rise quietly into the air and usually drop down again into the marsh a short distance away.

Jack snipe

February

A dog fox often lies up on drier ground in the centre of the marsh. Look for footprints in snow in the early morning and you will be able to see where the fox wandered from the reserve to forage in the town's dustbins at night.

March

Spring is in the air and hundreds of frogs start to spawn in the north and south pools. Herons often stand about in the centre of the marsh during the day, resting from fishing in the nearby river or for frogs in the pools.

March is perhaps the best time for siskins, although they are on the reserve all winter. These small finches, probably visitors from northern Europe, are common through the winter at Ipsley. Listen for flocks twittering in the distance as they feed in the alder trees, extracting the seeds from the small false-cones. Thousands of siskins spend the winter at Ipsley and this is one of the biggest regular flocks for miles around.

April

The anthills are very striking at this time of year. Crowned with violets they stand out on the drier parts of the marsh. The fairly well-drained environment on top of the anthill above the water-logged ground suits the flowers. There are hundreds of anthills, all active, although you rarely see the ants except on hot summer days when they come to the surface and enlarge the hill a little more. Some of the hills must be very old colonies. Other flowers which appreciate the hills follow the violets. Germander speedwell turns some hills bright blue, and others become yellow with lady's bedstraw. The ground between the hills is quite wet and covered with coarse grasses.

In mid-April the grasshopper warblers arrive. Up to eight pairs breed. Their extraordinary reeling song (likened to a sewing machine running) can be heard for long distances but is very directional making the birds difficult to locate. Look into the bramble patches and search for the open bright orange mouths of the singing birds.

May

Look for the herd of 9–12 cattle. The family which is resident on the marsh for most of the year give birth to their calves in dry secluded corners amongst long grass and scrub.

Many summer visiting warblers breed in the scrub and woodland including blackcaps, garden warblers, chiffchaffs and willow warblers. Bullfinches are common. Female cuckoos visit the marsh giving the bubbling call, but do not seem to stay to breed.

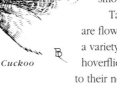

Cuckoo

June

The small, single leaves of adder's-tongue are quite common amongst the anthills and seem to be increasing.

Cuckoos visit the reserve to feed, hunting for hairy caterpillars amongst the grass which no other bird will eat. Their favourite

drinker and lappet moth caterpillars are common.

Crows are regularly seen and territorial boundary squabbles are not uncommon between the three resident pairs. Jays and great spotted woodpeckers can be seen in the woods.

July

Lots and lots of ringlet butterflies among the tall grasses and scrub. Hundreds can be seen, and day-flying burnet moths abound in the rough grassland.

Look out for the tall yellow spires of flowering agrimony. Daddy-long-legs (crane-flies) are abundant now and through most of the spring and summer.

August

This is the best time to look at the rushes for which the reserve is important. Six species have been found. In the pools stoneworts are abundant, and reedmace flower heads (often wrongly called bulrushes) are forming. This invasive plant has to be kept under control by regular pulling to prevent it taking over the pools completely and smothering all else.

Tall marsh thistles are flowering and attract a variety of bumble-bees, hoverflies and butterflies to their nectar-rich heads.

September

The best month for dragonflies. Fourteen species have been recorded. Big emperor dragonflies patrol territories along the pool edges and inspect human visitors

with care, often hovering a few inches in front of your face! Stand still by the shallow pools for a while and you will soon be 'buzzed'. Southern and migrant hawkers hunt for small insects.

Big, medium-sized and small bats feed over the marsh at dusk. Pipistrelles, long-eared bats and Daubenton's bat are seen, the latter swooping low over the pools.

Daubenton's bat

October

A hundred or more pied wagtails roost in the reedmace beds, dropping in at dusk to a place of safety over water. The first siskins of the winter arrive, and also wintering fieldfares and redwings.

November

Look for barn owls and short-eared owls which occasionally hunt for small field voles in the rough grassland on dull winter days. Flocks of magpies gather on the reserve, the record is over 60 in a tree, looking like strange exotic fruit!

December

Redwings and fieldfares visit the reserve, sometimes in thousands to feed on haws, and in the evening to roost in bushes and old hedges. Seeds from the berries they have eaten fall to the ground in their droppings and many germinate later in the year. Various cotoneasters, hollies and other berried plants appear beneath the trees but few survive in the shady conditions.

The resident tawny owl calls from the woods and may be disturbed during the day to be pestered by a mob of song birds.

The Knapp and Papermill

This reserve, at Alfrick, covers 26 hectares of old orchard, meadows, woods and 1 mile of the Leigh Brook. Knapp House lies at the entrance to the reserve where there is a small wildlife garden. The house is the warden's private residence. There is a small information lobby. The reserve is spread along a winding stream valley, with marshes, wet fields and an extensive flower-rich hay meadow which is grazed by cattle. The Papermill Meadow at the end of the reserve furthest from the Knapp House is rough grassland and scrub surrounded by woods.

From Worcester follow the A4103 Hereford road. Turn right at the small roundabout about ¾ mile after crossing Bransford Bridge over the River Teme, then left along the Bransford–Smith End Green–Alfrick Pound road. After about 3 miles the reserve entrance is on the left where the road crosses the Leigh Brook. There is limited parking near the bridge and a small parking space at the reserve entrance for disabled people only. This is also the access for residents of Knapp House and care must be taken not to cause an obstruction. Large parties should contact the warden via the Trust's office beforehand so that alternative parking arrangements can be made. The reserve is open at all times.

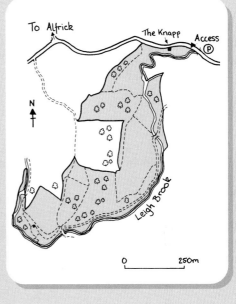

by *Colin and Heather Raven*

January 1993

The apple orchard is the first part of the reserve seen by most visitors. It is a typical old Worcestershire apple orchard of tall lichen-encrusted trees with spreading crowns. Now almost a hundred years old these trees usually still bear a good crop of fruit, mainly of Bramleys and Annie Elizabeths. Originally planted for cooking apples or for cider-making, nowadays most of the fruit is allowed to drop and is eaten by the local wildlife instead.

Standard fruit trees, which are now rarely seen, tend to be susceptible to wind-throw and our year commenced with a stormy week in January which brought down two of the oldest and largest trees. Unfortunately both fell into the Leigh Brook, the fast flowing tributary of the River Teme which runs through the reserve, making retrieval difficult and also resulting in part of the bank being washed away by the brook in full spate. The nest box warden, Garth Lowe, risked life and limb to rescue one of his boxes, a particular favourite with the nuthatches, which he safely relocated on another apple tree for the forthcoming season.

February

About half of the reserve's 26 hectares is woodland. These woodlands range greatly in character and composition, shaped by the underlying geology which changes completely within a matter of metres, and by the way they have been managed by man. Until about 50 years ago these woods were worked as coppice mainly to provide hop-poles, but also for firewood and various hazel products.

In recent years the Worcestershire Wildlife Trust has reinstated a programme of coppicing to restore the conditions created by this traditional form of woodland management, as these favour many wild flowers, butterflies and birds.

An area of about a fifth of a hectare (half an acre) is coppiced each winter. This winter's plot was felled in February. Winter is chosen as the best time to carry out

Early dog-violet

coppicing, when the trees and shrubs are dormant and so regrow more vigorously from their cut stumps. Also during winter there is less damage to wildlife as most wild flowers are dormant and the main breeding season for birds and wild animals is avoided. However, the early arrival of spring in 1993 meant that the leaves of bluebells were so well advanced that particular care was needed to remove the cut poles of lime, hazel, ash, oak and maple as quickly as possible.

As soon as the felling was completed, volunteers from the BTCV were on hand to plant new saplings where the original trees and shrubs had died back, thus helping to restore a full stock of trees for the future.

March

The early spring continued with primroses and violets flowering throughout the woodlands. By the second week of March it was warm enough on some days to encourage onto the wing the first of the season's butterflies. Peacock, small tortoiseshell, brimstone and comma were all seen.

By the end of the third week of March the frogs in the pond were noisily making their presence known to potential mates, and for that matter anyone else who went within 50 metres of their pond, now surrounded by the yellow blooms of marsh-marigold. This particular version of *son et lumiere* was enjoyed by those who joined us on our first guided walk of the year – part of a woodland management course organised by BTCV.

Common frog

The monthly work party concentrated on mowing a steep grassy bank to encourage patches of cowslips which have been spreading in recent years. This patch of the reserve was a favourite of Tom Graty, a dentist from Birmingham who had retired to a local village. In the last few years he became involved with the reserve and would visit, often several times a week, to help with wardening and other jobs. Tom adopted the cowslip bank and regularly cleared brambles. He always liked to help with the mowing and his photographs recorded the spread of 'his' cowslips. Sadly, he died last year and could not see his cowslips in full flower within a few weeks of the bank being mowed.

Toothwort

April

The Easter weekend marks the beginning of the main visitor season for the reserve. With two popular Bank Holidays in April and May around half of our 15,000 annual visitors come to the reserve in these two months. Such an influx brings its own problems. Usually the wildlife tolerates it all without noticeable effect but unfortunately in 1993 our kingfishers decided enough was enough and abandoned their nest on the reserve over the Easter Bank Holiday weekend. Careless behaviour by just a few people robbed thousands of careful and genuinely interested visitors of the

opportunity to see these beautiful birds from the small hide opposite the nest site. Fortunately the kingfishers nested further downstream and have since returned to their old nest site on the reserve.

By the end of April many of our summer visitors had arrived. Most prominent were the chiffchaffs, willow warblers and blackcaps which seem to occupy the same areas of the woods and even the same perches each year to declare and defend their territories, often favouring areas coppiced a few years earlier.

The monthly work party concentrated on repairing sections of the way-marked nature trail which forms a circuit through the meadows and woodlands. We worked on a steep section of the path which required new steps, beside the best colony of early-purple orchids on the reserve.

By late April the toothwort, a parasitic plant related to the broomrapes, is in flower. The best place to see it is by the old hazel trees in Daffodil Field. Toothwort depends on hazel roots for its food supply, lacking the energy-producing chlorophyll found in all green plants.

Orange-tip butterflies are frequently seen in the orchard, where the caterpillar's foodplant, cuckooflower, thrives. Nearby are cowslips and primroses which hybridise to produce false oxlips, which flower in April.

May

By May the woodlands are carpeted with wild flowers, especially in the areas coppiced in recent years. The bluebells alone are worth a visit, complemented by white stitchwort, red campion and yellow archangel: this natural outburst of colour is truly memorable. The spring wild flowers thrive in the open sunny conditions created by coppicing and bloom prolifically. As the coppice regrows during the following 20 years the flowers subside but have, in that time, laid down a bank of seed in the soil which will survive until the next time the coppice is cut to provide again the conditions for germination, so starting the whole cycle again.

Yellow archangel

One of the delights of being a 'live-in' warden is that you see the reserve at all times of the year and all times of day. An early morning walk in May produced the rare sight of a badger drinking from a puddle in Comfrey Field.

By mid-May the apple orchard is filled with the white heads of cow parsley growing under the trees. The range of wild flowers which grow here – some typical grassland plants, others from woodlands – makes the orchard a favourite place for butterflies. In May the green-veined whites are abundant.

Dan Asterley, a retired local teacher, has been fishing the Leigh Brook for over 50 years. No-one knows the brook better. He remembers when the otters were here, and since the early days he has recorded his observations on wildlife. Dan starts fishing for trout in May. He tells us there are very few mayflies this year, and the algae are bad. Even worse, the fish are small

and poor, but this could be due to the hot, dry spring.

By mid-May the biggest of the wild service-trees are in flower. At first sight they may be mistaken for elder bushes with their crowns of white flowers. Although common at the reserve the wild service-tree is a rare native tree of ancient woods.

June

By June, most of the reserve's eighty or so nest boxes are occupied. Whilst many are used by blue tits and great tits, some are taken by pied flycatchers. These have to be reserved for them each year by blocking the holes to stop the tits getting in. The trick is, of course, to remember to remove the blocks in time!

Meanwhile in the garden of the warden's house the spotted flycatchers are busily feeding on airborne insects using telegraph wires as hunting perches.

Big Meadow, originally called Great Epiphany Meadow, is a large wild flower meadow in the middle of the reserve. Each spring and early summer a succession of wild flowers grow up and bloom to form the hay which is cut in July. In June the meadow is yellow with buttercups, yellow-rattle and bird's-foot-trefoil. These contrast with the white of the oxeye daisies and the pink of the clover. Meanwhile the first of the common blue butterflies are on the wing.

Common blue

One of the wardens' jobs in June is to keep an eye on the orchids in Big Meadow and parts of the apple orchard. The tall, lilac-

flowered common spotted-orchids thrive in a particular part of the orchard flushed by limy springs. In 1993 the flower spike count here exceeded a hundred. They also did well in Big Meadow where they were found scattered throughout the field. Big Meadow also supports a colony of green-winged orchids, the most typical orchid of hay meadows in Worcestershire. This colony of up to 200 plants flowering in a year is gradually increasing and spreading through the meadow.

The end of June was very rainy, so much so that the lorry-load of fencing posts delivered to the reserve had to be dropped off at the warden's house because the fields were waterlogged. The rain also flattened the hay due to be cut in less than three weeks in Big Meadow. On the monthly work party we cleared brambles from around new trees and coppice growth in one of the coppice plots.

July

July was much warmer and sunnier than June and turned out to be a very good month for butterflies on the reserve. Both Papermill Meadow and Big Meadow change colour in July as the hay loses its vivid green-ness and the wild flowers and grasses ripen and fade. The yellows of the June flowers are replaced by the pink of knapweed. This year, the show of knapweed in Papermill Meadow was particularly prolific and complemented by many dainty blue harebells, the large pink flowers of mallow, and areas of bright pink centaury. On warm

sunny evenings we saw purple
hairstreak butterflies fluttering high
up in the oaks around the edges of
Papermill Meadow.

At the work party we worked in
Papermill Meadow pulling ragwort
plants by hand. If not controlled
these weeds can proliferate on dry
grasslands like the higher slopes of
the meadow.

The hay in Big Meadow was
cut on 21 July during a dry, sunny
spell. As it was being cut a white
admiral butterfly was seen in the
meadow. This species is an
infrequent visitor to the reserve,
so probably travels from a colony
somewhere on the Suckley Hills.

The hot weather continued
allowing the hay to be turned on
23 and baled on 27 July, all of the
bales being taken by the local
farmer.

August

August is the beginning of the
fruiting season on the reserve.
There are remnants of old plum
orchards with damsons and yellow
egg plums. No longer picked by
people these provide a good source
of food for many insects, mammals
and birds which feed upon them
either on the tree or after they have
fallen. However in 1993 plums were
very scarce with some trees bearing
no fruit at all. We believe this was
caused by late spring frosts.

This was the second season that
we had been unable to graze the
grassland under the trees in the
apple orchard. Teams of volunteers
from the local BTCV groups did
sterling work with an ageing Allen
Scythe and a dozen hay rakes. If we
do not mow the orchard it will
become progressively swamped by

coarse grasses and many of the wild
flowers would struggle to survive.

Unfortunately apple orchards
are a favoured by wasps and our
mowers uncovered a very active
nest in the ground, bringing
aggressive and painful retaliation
resulting in excessive consumption
of "waspeze" from the first-aid kit.
However within a few days we
noticed that the uncovered nest had
been dug out from the ground and
all but a few wasps had
disappeared. The work of local
badgers we believe.

In the wildlife garden, the
buddleia bush was in full flower,
attracting butterflies in profusion.
Peacocks, small tortoiseshells, red
admirals, and occasional painted
ladies provided a colourful display.
The herbaceous border has been
planted so that during every month

between February and October there are plants in flower to provide a source of nectar for insects, starting with the primulas and polyanthus and ending with Michaelmas daisies. There are plenty of berry-bearing shrubs to provide food and shelter for all sorts of wildlife in the autumn, and thistles, burdocks and teasels which bear large seed heads which attract finches. There is a small pond and a small wild flower meadow which is cut for hay in July or August. There are resident grass snakes and slow-worms which keep the slugs and snails at bay.

September

Like spring, autumn also came early and the trees started to change colour during September. Because of the variety of different trees on the reserve the autumn colours are quite spectacular. The maple family are all known for their vivid autumn shades and the native field maple, found throughout the woodlands, is no exception. Its colours are however rivalled by the even brighter oranges and reds of the leaves of the wild service-trees.

This is the time of year when the squirrels become much more visible, taking nuts from the trees and bushes. They are especially keen on hazelnuts and the reserve contains some very old hazel trees, especially those alongside the brook in Daffodil Meadow.

October

October is a quiet time on the reserve. The summer migrants have flown to their winter grounds and most of the winter birds have yet to arrive. The trees are losing their leaves and most of the apples in the orchard have dropped to the floor. On sunny days red admirals feed on the fallen fruit and closer inspection reveals a variety of chew marks and peck marks. The orchard is filled with the smell of cider created by natural yeasts which ferment the fallen fruits.

The reserve has lost its vibrant summer and autumn colours. The woodlands are shades of brown and grey interrupted only by occasional evergreen plants such as yew and holly and the vivid orange and pink fruit heads of the spindle.

This is the season for fungi. There are large fairy rings appearing in Big Meadow. These are created by underground fungi which grow outwards forming a complete ring of lush green grass. During October toadstools, the fruiting bodies of the fungus, form and scatter spores. In the woodlands some of the old coppice stools bear large bracket fungi. A walk in the woodlands usually reveals a good variety of fungi including stinkhorns, inkcaps and earthstars. Dead and decaying timber on the ground supports an array of tiny and colourful rusts and moulds. Nothing on the reserve is wasted – it is all used and recycled by the wildlife itself, maintaining the balance of nature.

The reserve was one of several chosen for English Nature's Dormouse Recovery Scheme. This small and elusive mammal has been recorded on the reserve several times in the past, usually when discovered hibernating in one of the bird boxes. This year a dozen or so specially designed boxes for dormice were put up on an area of old hazel coppice: the dormouse's favourite habitat. It often makes its hibernation nest in old large coppice stools so this is why the area was chosen. In 1994 at least one box was occupied.

November

The winter birds have started to arrive. On cold frosty mornings redwings and fieldfares visit the orchard and Big Meadow to feed on fallen fruit. This is often a good time to see wildlife as the cover of leaves has disappeared and the search for food brings the wildlife out into the open.

Earthstar

At the end of February we welcomed some special visitors to the reserve: 14 head of cattle from a local farm. It had been two years since we had last seen cattle on the meadows. In this time Papermill Meadow had grown tall and rank but to our great surprise (and relief) our bovine friends soon chewed away most of the matted grass (which the local farmer described as 'feggy') to reveal the old anthills and contours of the field. Unfortunately they also took a liking to anything green in the surrounding woodlands and the wardens spent much of February and March herding young cattle back into the meadow and repairing the fences. Over the Christmas holidays our daily head count increased by one thanks to the birth of a new calf witnessed by Heather and Matthew. This made up for the loss of a heifer earlier in the month which we discovered lying dead by the brook one Saturday morning. The reason for this was never discovered.

Stinkhorn

Buzzards are resident in the valley of the Leigh Brook all year round and whenever you visit the reserve there is a good chance of seeing them, usually one or two, but sometimes more of these majestic birds of prey congregate in the skies above us. On several occasions during the Jubilee Year we saw up to six, and on one memorable day in the previous year 11 were seen.

December

The Leigh Brook is perhaps the most prominent natural feature of the reserve. Its actions have over time created the steep valley sides which are now clothed in rich woodland. It rises on the western side of the Malvern Hills near Colwall, and flows into the River Teme at Leigh. Its course runs virtually south to north and the reserve is situated over the section where it cuts through the limestone of the Suckley Hills.

Despite the increased burden of pollution in recent years it remains one of the cleanest waters in the county, allowing it to support rich fauna and flora. It is well-known by fishermen for its brown trout, which have attracted wild otters to once again visit the reserve, having been absent for most of the last three decades. The resident kingfishers are a favourite with visitors and grey wagtails usually nest on a ledge on Pivany Bridge. But the brook's tranquil summer flow can turn into a raging torrent after heavy rainfall, and flooding of local fields, woods and roads is common in the winter and spring. On the reserve this has for several years caused a particular problem, regularly washing away part of our only access track. The advice and help of the National Rivers Authority was sought and in January 1993 they created a flood defence bank along a section of the brook. While carrying out this work the NRA staff were lucky enough to catch a glimpse of a dipper, once a regular sight on the reserve, but driven out in recent years by increased pollution levels. Let us hope that dippers will return before too long.

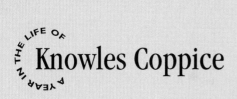
Knowles Coppice

This 7½ hectare reserve contains mature sessile oak woodland, two small meadows and about 400 metres of the Dowles Brook. The main block of woodland is situated on a small plateau of acidic soils overlooking the brook, with a further long strip on steep stream-side banks. The two small meadows have more basic soils deposited by the brook, and the one situated on the north side of the Dowles Brook is actually in Shropshire.

Knowles Coppice lies in the heart of Wyre Forest near Lodge Hill Farm, residence of the National Nature Reserve warden. Follow the A456 Bewdley to Tenbury Wells road up the hill from the centre of the town. Turn right into The Lakes Road and follow roads through the housing estate to Dry Mill Lane. This lane leads down into the forest. The best way to enjoy the forest and the reserve is to park here and walk. There is very little parking space. Near the bottom of the lane, by the old railway bridge abutments, take the left turn and head west on to the old railway line and head for Lodge Hill Farm. The reserve is open at all times to members of the Trust. Non-members must first obtain a permit from the Trust's office.

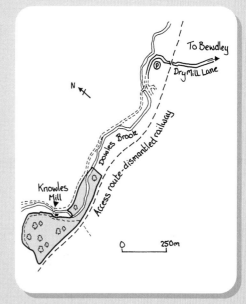

by Roger Robinson, Chris Bradley and Sylvia Sheldon

To know Knowles Coppice through the seasons is to learn something of the slow rhythm of the life in the Wyre Forest. The wood has changed much in the last couple of generations, but it remains a beautiful and ecologically important place. The majority of the trees in the wood are sessile oaks with some birch, holly and planted larch. Cowslip, devils'-bit scabious, common valerian and wood club-rush grow in the meadows. Dowles Brook is an unpolluted natural stream where dippers, grey wagtails and kingfishers are often seen.

Grey wagtail

January 1993
Dog foxes are heard barking through the woods. Resident birds begin pair bonding. Woodpeckers start drumming towards the end of the of month. Honeysuckle leaf buds start to open.

February
On warm days wood ants begin to forage and repair their nests. Reptiles begin to stir from their winter torpor. Kingfishers, grey wagtails and dippers start establishing territory. The tearing alarm calls of agitated mistle thrushes can be heard.

March
In March it seems that the woodland has overslept, for the oaks are still bare when the surrounding landscape is full of the bright greens of the season. The calls of migrant birds (chiffchaff and blackcap are the first to arrive) reassure us that spring is coming. Celandines, anemones, violets and other early flowers benefit from the late emergence of leaves in the woodland canopy. As soon as the temperature reaches 13°C brimstone butterflies appear, seeming impossibly bright amidst the white of the frosts that linger in the steep valley of the Dowles. Peacocks, commas and small tortoiseshells soon follow. Reptiles can be seen basking on sunny banks, and on mild evenings hedgehogs appear. The pace of life is quickening.

April

A colourful month, with primroses and cuckooflowers out; and speckled wood, green-veined white, small white, holly blue and orange-tip butterflies on the wing. Grass snakes are mating, and the fallow deer bucks begin casting their antlers. More migrant birds arrive, notably pied flycatchers, cuckoos, redstarts, swallows and house martins.

May

Mallard ducklings scurry along the Dowles Brook, following their parents. Spotty fledgling robins appear in the gardens. Pearl-bordered fritillaries, skippers, and meadow browns take to the wing, and so do several species of damselfly. Common spotted-orchids, twayblades, bluebells, and

cowslips are in flower, as is the blackthorn.

June

Fallow deer fawns are born. Tiny froglets leave the ponds, and can be seen on the bare ground of the forest tracks. Pied flycatchers and redstarts are beginning to fledge. Fallow bucks start to grow their antlers again.

Redstart

July

The time to look for silver-washed and the increasingly rare high brown fritillaries. White admirals are occasionally seen, and gatekeepers are usually plentiful.

Betony, musk mallow and St John's-worts are in bud, if not already in bloom.

August

High summer sunlight filters through the thick canopy to dapple the bracken which has now hidden much of the ground. Caterpillars hang in mid-air, apparently defying gravity. They have 'baled out' of the canopy, suspended by a fine silk thread, to avoid a foraging bird. In the heat of noon, the woods become almost still, with perhaps the cry of a buzzard high above to break the silence. Sneezewort, devils'-bit scabious and harebell come into flower. The lizards and slow-worms

give birth. Dippers begin singing again, having stopped during nesting, presumably to reinforce their territories.

September
Fallow bucks have now grown their hard antlers and the first groaning calls of the rut can be heard. Many different fungi appear, from the unappealing but edible beefsteak to the eerily beautiful but deadly destroying angel. Swallows are congregating for the return flight to South Africa, and the adders are giving birth.

October
Autumn often seems to rise out of the ground in Wyre. The bracken

Betony

begins to turn yellow, and the leaves of wood sage fade to russet. Soon the changes rise into the silver birch and hazel branches, and finally into the oak canopy. Late-flowering plants such as toadflax, betony, and hawkbit attract the last butterflies.

Deer-watching now becomes the priority as the rut is in full swing. Mixed flocks of tits or finches sweep through the woods, as the forest braces itself for winter.

November
Catkins appear on alder and birch branches. The woodland management of felling and coppicing begins. Wood

pigeons hunt for acorns in large groups. The dog foxes begin barking again.

December
The quiet visitor can often see secretive bullfinches feeding on haws. The bare ground and tree branches make it easier to see deer and other animals, but it is much harder to approach them unseen.

One of the delights of Knowles Coppice is that there is always something to see. It may be no more than a great tit trying to fight the rival it can see in the mirror of a forester's tractor, or one may be rewarded by the sight of the rare land caddisfly, or perhaps a pair of fallow bucks sparring. The learning process never ends.

Lion Wood

This 3 hectare wood was purchased jointly by the Worcestershire and Warwickshire Wildlife Trusts in 1982. It lies at Portway near the west side of the A435 about 3 miles north of Redditch, and just on the Worcestershire side of the boundary between the two counties. Lion Wood lies on a low ridge of well-leached glacial drift acid soils. The principal trees are oak, birch, rowan and holly with some alder buckthorn in the understorey. The ground flora contains plants which prefer acid conditions, such as bilberry and wood sage. This woodland community is of a type which is uncommon in Worcestershire.

The wood is open at all times. The main A435 dual carriageway bypasses Portway at its junction with Brockhill Lane. Access is via a gate on the old road at SP 085717. The White Lion pub marked on older maps near the gate has been demolished.

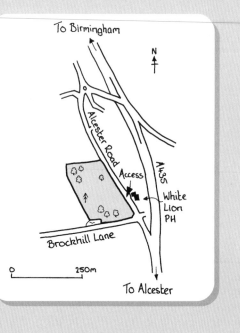

by Tony Jackson

The wood is rather a dark place with an unusual understorey of holly and rowan. Where the drooping branches of holly touch the ground they become covered with leaf litter and take root, so extending the understorey by layering. There are extensive stands of rowan in places. The woodland floor carries a fairly small range of plants. The wood was once more open and heathy, with heather and bilberry. Under the shade of the oaks these plants are now rather tall, lank and not growing well.

Bilberry

Spring

This is probably the most attractive time to visit the wood. As the tree leaves open birds are in full song. The wood supports a good community of woodland birds including great and blue tits, probably four pairs of nuthatches, treecreepers, and both great and lesser spotted woodpeckers.

There are plenty of dead branches on the trees which supply invertebrate food for the birds and, as they decay, nest holes. Summer visitors are blackcaps and chiffchaffs.

Brimstone butterflies are quite common, their caterpillars feeding on the leaves of alder buckthorn.

Summer

Deep shade in the wood. Most activity is in the canopy where the tits and warblers feed amongst the leaves on moth caterpillars. The thin layer of bramble and bracken on the woodland floor is often shaded out by the encroaching holly. Although quite frequent the alder buckthorn does not grow well in the shade. Blackbirds and song thrushes are attracted to feed on the rowan berries as they ripen in July and August.

Autumn and winter

There is a large roost of redwings, fieldfares and wood pigeons and the birds can be seen moving into the wood as dusk falls. The holly provides good protection from the weather and hides the roosting birds from predators. During the day tit flocks move through the wood in their endless search for food: look out for the accompanying treecreepers and nuthatches.

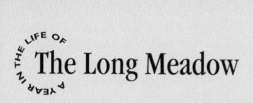
The Long Meadow

Long Meadow is a permanent pasture lying by the Piddle Brook near Radford, about ½ mile south of Inkberrow. It was given to the Trust in 1972. The turf contains many plants typical of old lowland meadows, including cowslips, adder's-tongue fern and green-winged orchids. The bank overlooking the meadow is covered with mixed scrubland and its berries attract many thrushes to feed in winter. The meadow is managed as a hay meadow, being cut late in summer and then grazed in autumn and early winter.

Long Meadow is ½ mile south of Inkberrow adjacent to the Piddle Brook. Access is via public footpaths. Leave the Flyford Flavell to Weethley Gate road west of Goom's Hill Farm. Because of difficult access over farmland this reserve is only open to members and non-members who have obtained a special permit from the Trust's office.

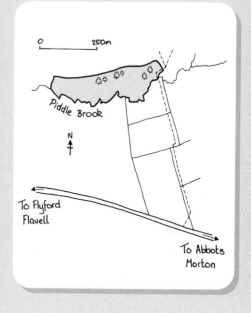

by Elisabeth Jackson

January-March 1993

Whether the winter is mild or severe, all the hawthorn berries in the reserve are finished by New Year. There are many hawthorn bushes: the ones which cover a bank adjoining the strip of woodland are big and old and could be described as trees.

In the 1940s this was an open bank with tall grasses and the flowers of field scabious and restharrow. Marbled white butterflies bred here. Dotted about in the grass were tiny hawthorn bushes. As the bushes grew they smothered the flowers and grass, so we lost the beautiful butterflies.

Comma

However, years later, in 1976, I had a pleasant surprise – a marbled white appeared from somewhere and fed for a long time on a flower of spear thistle.

Now, with hedgerows closely shaved by mechanical means, or removed altogether, the hawthorns provide valuable food for the birds.

In March a day comes which 'unlocks' the hibernating butterflies, and occasionally I see all four of the hibernating species on the same date. 13 March is one of those days. The weather is superb. My first brimstone hastens along the edge of what we call "The Bushes" (the band of hawthorn trees). The first peacock basks in the sun by two large logs, the remains of a fallen oak. A little further along a small tortoiseshell rests among the yellow flowers of lesser celandine at the edge of the wood. On a bank towards the public footpath, a glowing comma spreads its wings in the warmth.

April-June

4 April is not a fine enough day for butterflies to be out, but I don't want to miss seeing the blackthorn in flower. Sure enough, the blackthorn thicket is a mass of white blossom, though there are very few insects about to visit it.

By 26 April the cowslips are at their best. In the grass I find several large somewhat irregularly-shaped mushrooms, with thick fleshy cap and stem uniformly cream-coloured. These are St George's mushrooms.

During the eighteen years I have been recording in the reserve they have appeared just once before – in May 1978.

30 April. A fine day is forecast, too good to miss. At the reserve one of my favourite insects is about – the tiny, jewel-like small yellow underwing moth. I like its simple life history: the caterpillar feeds on mouse-ear chickweed, and the moth flies on sunny days in May and early June in grass-bordered lanes and hay meadows.

Sixteen green-winged orchids (our speciality) are in flower and adder's-tongue fern is abundant in the same area.

Until last year willow warblers nested here. It is sadly quiet without them. For once I have not even heard a chiffchaff, pausing with us on its migration.

By 18 May the pasture is a solid yellow carpet of meadow buttercups. The little misshapen goldilocks grows here too. It is plentiful beside the stream and flowers in April. Up the public footpath I see interesting insects: a speckled wood butterfly, one of the striking red-and-black froghopper bugs, a scorpionfly and several different hoverflies.

Long-tailed tits are often to be seen, minutely exploring the hedges. On 15 June a family of ten comes close, eight of them alighting on a small dead tree above my head, where they preen busily. The 23 is

a red-letter day: a chiffchaff has appeared, and calls much of the time that I am in the reserve.

July–September

5 July. By the bushes an attractive group of five tall stems of hairy St John's-wort, with many flowers and buds, shows up well against a background of dark foliage. This plant has appeared twice before, in 1981 and 1982.

On a bank close to the bushes are handsome flowers of woolly thistle; one flower is about 6 cm across, and is visited by two white-tailed bumble bees and a hoverfly, all on it together.

Hairy St John's-wort

This plant appeared for the first time in 1968. Jeff, our warden, had been helping on a reserve where it grows, so we think a seed may have been brought here inadvertently.

22 July, 9.15 a.m. This morning I am able to add gatekeeper to my list of butterflies. Later in the day the meadow is mown, and on 1 August the hay is baled and most of it taken away in two enormous loads. By the time I go, on 10 August, the last bales have gone and the reserve is a neat uniformly green meadow.

In 1976 I noticed that on the oaks a few of the acorns were strangely deformed by an emerald-green growth which resembled the

Knopper gall

inside of a walnut. A newspaper article enabled me to identify this as the knopper gall, *Cynips quercus-calicis*, a newcomer spreading up from the south. Each year since, it has appeared in the reserve in varying quantities, but this year the oaks are covered with it as never before. There is scarcely a normal acorn on the trees.

October–December

15 October. In the reserve the ash trees are yellow, the oaks and hawthorns tawny. By the gate a single branch of hawthorn has wine-red leaves and sprays of crimson berries.

8 November. A jay calls and several fieldfares drift from the streamside bushes. Further along,

the spindle bush is shedding red leaves. There are still a few berries: the rose-pink cases have split revealing orange-coloured seeds.

In the stream a moorhen scuttles to cover, leaving ever-widening ripples on the water. It is good news to have a moorhen in the reserve. Several pairs used to nest along the stream until mink invaded this area.

1 December is mild with long sunny intervals and I seize the opportunity to visit the reserve. Most of the berries have gone now, but a few redwings and fieldfares fly from the bushes giving their distinctive calls.

On the way back I notice cowslip leaves and the pleated leaves of salad burnet – the year has turned full-circle.

The Marsh Warbler Reserves and Nafford Island

Worcestershire has for many years been the stronghold of breeding marsh warblers in the British Isles, with over 100 pairs nesting in the county in the 1970s (25% on the Trust's reserves). Unfortunately Worcestershire's birds have been declining since the early 1980s and now only 2-8 pairs nest annually. The reasons for the decline are, despite five years of research, not understood. It is likely that the birds suffered excessive mortality either on migration or in their African winter quarters and this, together with a general decrease in suitable habitat in their preferred part of Worcestershire, has caused the decline.

Access to marsh warbler reserves is restricted. Nafford Island, which held marsh warblers long ago, is crossed by a public footpath leading from the Eckington to Great Comberton road (SO 942417), across the sluice gates, lock, island and weir, to Birlingham. Remember, the river is dangerous and visitors must take care. Children and dogs must be kept under control. There is a little parking space on the roadside. Fishing is not permitted from the island. Please keep to the footpaths, especially during spring and summer, to avoid damaging the tall vegetation.

Marsh warbler

The Trust manages several small pieces of land beside the River Avon primarily for marsh warblers although the sites also contain a rich variety of wildlife. The reserves typically contain beds of nettles, great willowherb and meadowsweet together with willows, old hedges and scattered small trees. The ground is usually wet underfoot. There are many other birds including reed and sedge warblers, reed buntings, and most common birds. They also contain a wide variety of plants and abundant insects. Most are remnants of abandoned wet fields, old osier beds, or riverside waste ground.

The Trust monitors all its marsh warbler reserves, and also other sites once used by the birds, every year. For the last five years John Hodson has been our marsh warbler man and his accounts of his experiences have

delighted readers of the Trust's newsletter *Worcestershire Wildlife News*. John's 1993 account is reprinted here to give a flavour of the problems of marsh warbler conservation.

Marsh warbler reserves
by John Hodson

Regular readers of *Worcestershire Wildlife News* will be aware of the many and varied problems that have kept me awake at night. Apart from the usual risks from rain, wind and flood (even excessive heat on one occasion) I have been troubled by magpies, crows, the close proximity of irrigation sprayers, explosive bird scarers and bird of prey kites. The last couple of seasons have been the 'rabbit years', with large numbers of these animals eating their way

through the nettle beds, and goosegrass has always been a problem. Although all these things have been a great worry to me, the whole catalogue of previous problems has paled into insignificance compared with this year's episodes.

This year's 'problems' were intent on one thing only and that was to rob any marsh warblers nest that could be found. Yes, we have been visited by that delightful creature, the egg collector, not once but probably on five occasions by four different sets of individuals.

One clutch of eggs was taken a couple of days before hatching was due, rendering them useless to egg collectors. Two other nests were lost almost certainly to egg collectors and possibly one other. Despite this, some pairs bred successfully, but we decided that the actual numbers of present should not be made public.

I can hear Trust members asking how egg collectors managed to rob the nests while they were being wardened. Well, I can tell you they had an awful lot of luck. The first visit was to a site that contained only a singing unpaired male. I deliberately do not enter any of the sites both to avoid damage to the vegetation and disturbance to the birds. This site had metre-wide tracks systematically trampled throughout the vegetation indicating that the perpetrators had no idea whether nests were present or not, or where they might be. However the site from which the eggs were taken had only narrow access tracks which led almost directly to the nest site. Nothing was seen of the first lot of robbers but others were seen acting suspiciously by a colleague at another site. He found their car, and apparently they came from Devon.

A few days later at 05.30 one morning I was walking along the edge of a site when my dog indicated that something was in the ditch underneath the overgrown hedge. Thinking it to be a rabbit I sent her in. I heard twigs cracking and could see her tail wagging. Now tail wagging does not mean rabbit or fox but a potential stick thrower. She came out looking pleased and I knew that there was someone in there. After hearing more twigs crack I decided to go in. As I entered the ditch I immediately saw a figure in full camouflage clothing. (Does camouflage clothing ever work?) Wishing to engage him in conversation I moved towards him. He ran off down the ditch and I followed. On leaving the ditch I attempted to attract his attention with a large monopod I happened to be carrying, this startled him and he fell over. I also tripped at this point, just

as he got up to run off, but not before I made a further attempt to attract his attention. Excuses – well it was a ploughed field; I was wearing waders; it was 05.30 in the morning; he was much younger than me; and, yes, he got away!

The fourth incident involved a character who so fitted my idea of what an egg collector would (should!) look like that I could not believe he was one. He was not actually in one of the reserves but he looked suspicious and was not on a public footpath so I had a few words with him, and eventually he left. Next day I discovered he had been looking for turtle dove nests (he had actually told a dog-walker that!). Later that day I met him again and had a few more words with him. It turns out that he is a known collector and he lives within the region.

The colour ringed male marsh warbler red over blue, ringed as an adult in 1985, returned again this year, making him at least nine years old. Unfortunately he again failed to attract a female in spite of arriving earlier than usual. And some young marsh warblers did indeed fledge.

Nafford Island

Nafford Island lies between lock and weir in the River Avon near Birlingham. The lock is in regular use, especially by holiday boats in summer. Nearby are large sluice gates which are used to control the water level in the river. The island is roughly triangular and bordered by tall, almost vertical earth banks downstream of both the lock and weir. The third

upstream bank is lower with a marshy fringe where the river flows slowly towards the top of the weir.

In summer the island is covered with tall dense herbage, mainly nettles, cleavers, cow parsley and hemlock, with only a few wet patches of marshland containing meadowsweet and purple-loosestrife. There are a few pollarded willows on the river bank, willow scrub, elder and a dense thicket of blackthorn. Bur-reed, true bulrush, and yellow water-lilies fringe the upstream bank. The National Rivers Authority recently built an eel-path alongside the weir to enable eels to migrate upstream.

The island was once a marsh warbler breeding site but has not been used for many years. Sedge warblers, reed warblers and reed buntings do occur. Grey wagtails, which are more often associated with upland streams, nest, and kingfishers, mute swans, mallards and moorhens also occur. The blackthorn thicket is used by roosting birds of many species.

Otters have been seen near the island in recent years. They seem to be re-colonising Worcestershire from the upper reaches of the Rivers Severn and Teme and making their way back to old haunts along the River Avon. In summer the River Avon seems to be a fairly placid river, but it is full of muddy deeps and under-currents, and the flow from the weir is fast and dangerous. The river also carries treated sewage from many places upstream. Children visiting the island should be closely supervised.

Otter

Mill Meadow

Mill Meadow, near Drakes Broughton, is a 1 hectare meadow managed by the Trust. The meadow is owned by Mr Percy Cull, one of the generation of growers who made the Vale of Evesham famous for its fruit and vegetable production.

Access is restricted. Those wishing to visit the reserve must first obtain a permit from the Trust's office.

Devils'-bit scabious

by Stuart Corbett

Percy Cull, and his wife Hilda, are the third generation of Culls to farm in Drakes Broughton, and they have a fund of stories about life on the land over eighty years. Produce was sold on their market stall in the old Shambles Market Hall in Worcester for many years.

From the age of five Percy helped his father look after the crops and take them into Worcester by horse and cart. The family owned two waggon horses and they were kept on the Mill Meadow. Because of its value as grazing land the meadow has not been ploughed for at least three generations. It has also remained undrained and is thus a relict of old meadow land. The meadow is in the category of a clearing in mature oak woodland.

The woodland shelters the meadow from the prevailing winds, providing calm, warm conditions.

The southern half of the meadow is extremely wet during all of the winter, and most of the spring. Pools of water form in the furrows remaining from past 'ridge and furrow' cultivation. This may seem surprising after a superficial examination of the soil type, which is relatively sandy at the surface. However, digging down just a short way reveals the presence of sticky Lower Lias clays which inhibit the drainage.

On the southern side of the meadow is a small pond, situated between woodland and three large willows. Pollarding of the willows in December allows more light to reach the pond. The woodland edge near the pond appears to be a favourite feeding area for parties of blue and long-tailed tits during January. Coal tits are also seen, hiding food in the bark of the pollarded willows,

Goldcrests and treecreepers frequent the opposite edge of the meadow. There is a large amount of blackthorn in this area and a thorough search of young shoots was made in the hope of finding eggs of the brown hairstreak butterfly; however, none were found.

The flora of the meadow is clearly divided into two types. At the northern end of the reserve is a narrow strip dominated by coarse grasses such as timothy, rough

Goldcrest

meadow-grass and cock's-foot. This flora may be associated with the past feeding of hay to horses. The rest of the reserve has a richer flora. In early April the first leaves of the common spotted-orchid were noted amongst the finer grasses of the southern end of the meadow. During the rest of the month spring flowers such as dog-violet, primrose, bluebell and bugle put on a good show.

Invertebrates were becoming more active in sunny periods between the showers. The devil's coach-horse beetle was found, along with a number of ground beetles, beneath rotting wood in the woodland edge. Pockets of warm air form in the scalloped edges of the wood during sunny weather and these were much appreciated by the St Mark's fly, which is always common at the end of April.

Blue and great tits nested in boxes during May. A pair of great spotted woodpeckers took up residence in the meadow and these were seen on most visits during the rest of the summer. Chiffchaffs, cuckoos and swifts were also recorded this month.

Butterflies did not appear in large numbers but orange-tip, peacock and speckled wood were seen. Other insects were more active at the end of the month, with damselflies being common and shield bugs being particularly noticeable. Two species, *Syromastes marginatus* and *Pentatoma prasina*, made up the bulk of sightings.

Spotted-orchids were in full bloom during early June. This was a very good year and a count of approximately 700 spikes was made. Orchids were not found in

the area of coarser grasses in the north of the field.

In July the pond was completely covered in pondweed. Some of this was raked out and newts were found to be present.

During August devils'-bit scabious in flower. This plant, though still present in good numbers, may be suffering from the lack of grazing in the meadow in the recent past. In order to overcome this the Trust mows the meadow in the late summer. This operation usually results in some interesting sightings. A common lizard was seen basking on an anthill, and the nest of a harvest mouse was found in the area of taller grasses. The presence of these species indicate the importance of even a small reserve as both are uncommon nowadays in Worcestershire.

Monkwood

Monkwood is a 61 hectare ancient woodland. Originally a coppice-with-standards woodland, much of it was clear-felled 30–40 years ago, and then managed to produce small round-wood for the Harris Brush Co. near Bromsgrove. The wood contains many native tree species and also planted sycamore, Norway maple, and beech (not a typical tree of the wet poorly drained soils of Monkwood). Monkwood is divided by a minor road. The southern part, Little Monkwood, is owned jointly by the Trust and Butterfly Conservation. The larger northern part is owned by the Trust and managed in consultation with Butterfly Conservation. The two societies have worked well together in the wood which is particularly good for butterflies.

The entrance to the wood is on the minor road from the A443 near Grimley to Monkwood Green, where the road passes through the wood about 2 miles west of Grimley. On the north side of the road a track leads immediately into a small car park. There is a good system of paths and rides. Please keep dogs under control.

by Claire Turner and Mike Williams

March 1993

March can often prove a strange month weatherwise with very contrasting conditions. Silver Jubilee year proved no different with snow on the 1st followed by several days of cold and frosty conditions. Fortunately, this did not last long and the first signs of spring were not far away. The early brimstone butterflies, with their bright, sulphur-yellow wings, stirred from their deep winter slumber on 13th when temperatures soared to over 15°C, and they were soon joined by small tortoiseshells, commas and peacocks.

Chiffchaff

March also marks the month when the summer bird visitors begin to arrive and chiffchaffs are always the first to announce their presence, this year on 14th. Over at the ponds, smooth newts and the specially protected great crested newts return to the water, and pond-skaters and back-swimmers are seen. Plant life is still limited, except in very early seasons, but blackthorn blossom and pussy willows stand out against a backdrop of the bare leafless trees, while on the woodland floor a shimmer of white tinged with pink indicates that wood anemones are coming into flower.

March is always capable of throwing a surprise or two and a female large white butterfly on 25th was the earliest ever recorded in the Midlands.

April

Monkwood is especially noted for its early-purple orchids, which flower towards the end of April. Each year the number of spikes are monitored and this year 153 blooms were found, the highest count so far. April is also one of the best months for bird watching, with many species establishing territories and nest building. Blackcaps, garden warblers, whitethroats and especially willow warblers are all present in good numbers. Many visitors also listen for the first cuckoo which always arrives this month.

An evening visit is often worthwhile at this season of the year, as there is hope of seeing roding woodcock. Curlews still breed in the surrounding fields and their evocative, echoing calls can often be heard in April. Barn owls are now scarce in the county but occasionally show up on Monkwood Green adjacent to the wood where there are mice and voles.

May

Because there are so few old and decaying trees in Monkwood nest boxes have been erected for hole-nesting birds. The absence of old trees in the wood also affects bats and 11 boxes have been specially erected for their benefit. The tiny pipistrelle is the main species to benefit so far, although great tits are uninvited guests.

Spring flowers are normally at their peak during the first half of the month when bluebells attract many visitors. It is fortunate that Monkwood has a good system of hard-topped rides, making it very suitable for those with walking difficulties. The wood has been long known for its lilies-of-the-valley and they have benefited from the re-introduction of coppicing. The coppice plots are now a blaze of colour with ragged-Robin and stitchwort mixed in with ramsons, yellow archangel and wood spurge. Monkwood's trees and shrubs also look very attractive at this time of year with wild cherry, guelder-rose and wild service-tree all in flower.

Perhaps above all else Monkwood is renowned for its butterflies. No fewer than 36 species

Lily-of-the-valley

have been recorded in the last 15 years making it one of the top sites in the county. Most important of all is the delicate wood white, which is a national rarity, but is now seen in excellent numbers within the specially managed rides and coppices. Normally first seen in the second half of May, it has a slow, hesitant flight which can nevertheless, as frustrated photographers will testify, be remarkably persistent. The presence of the wood white attracts butterfly buffs from far and near and a sunny weekend in May or June often means a full car park.

Guelder-rose

June

Over the years, Monkwood has hosted a variety of special events and visits. The Royal Forestry Society, the RSPB, local hospitals, naturalists' societies and many others all visited the wood during Silver Jubilee year and were able to take part in guided walks led by members of the reserve management committee. On 1st June, the wood played host to the Land Rover UK Butterfly Check organised by Butterfly Conservation to mark their 25th anniversary which they share with the Trust. Despite rather dull and overcast conditions, the wood white was the commonest butterfly on the wing.

Amongst other noticeable insects in June are the dragonflies which are regularly seen around the ponds and elsewhere in the wood. Back in 1986, when Monkwood was acquired as a

nature reserve, there was a shortage of pools in the wood and one of the first projects tackled by the management committee was the creation of two ponds. These were immediately successful and, with help from a local plant hire firm, a much larger third pond has been completed. This last pond, complete with its own island, was designed with a series of bays to increase the opportunities for male dragonflies to establish their territories and so boost the number of dragonflies the pond can support. Already some 15 different species have been recorded, including the magnificent emperor dragonfly which is now breeding here.

The vicinity of the pools is also a good place to look for reptiles. Grass snakes are still relatively common, in fact years ago the wood used to be known by locals as "Snake Wood". Despite their harmless nature, grass snakes are often persecuted and do not like disturbance.

During June birds are increasingly preoccupied raising families and are not so easily seen, although this month buzzards have been much in evidence soaring and calling over the wood. It is good to see such a magnificent bird making a strong comeback in the county after several years of scarcity.

July

Weekly counts of butterflies are made throughout the summer and, even after seven years of recording, new species are occasionally seen.

A case in point was the white-letter hairstreak seen on the 2nd. This species, as a caterpillar, feeds on elm trees and has been badly affected by Dutch elm disease. Two other striking butterflies recorded during July are the white admiral and silver-washed fritillary. The white admiral was not seen at Monkwood until the mid-eighties, after a gap of almost 40 years, but it is now generally common. The bright orange silver-washed fritillary is less common but, with careful management, numbers are slowly increasing.

The rides at this time of year are particularly colourful with melilot, betony, musk mallow, knapweed and meadowsweet all in flower, while yellow loosestrife is a feature around the ponds. Another striking plant is the tall pendulous sedge which flourishes on damp clay soils.

The highlight of the summer at Monkwood occurred on 25th when, after months of planning and preparation, our reserve Open Day took place. In celebration of Silver Jubilee year and the return of otters to the county, we were pleased to welcome Daphne Neville and her two pet otters. Many hundreds of visitors passed through Monkwood during the day. Despite the heavy demand placed on our small band of volunteers, the enthusiastic reactions of visitors, perhaps seeing Monkwood for the first time, made the day very worthwhile.

Pendulous sedge

August

July and August are the busiest months for insects. Butterflies catch the eye by day, but for sheer quantity it is those custodians of the night, the moths, which win hands down. Running an ultraviolet light to attract moths has been a regular feature at Monkwood for many years and the total number of species of moths now tops the 500 mark. It is always well worth looking for the earlier stages of butterflies and moths and a search of rosebay willowherb along the main ride on 14th produced a larva of the elephant hawk moth. When disturbed this striking caterpillar is able to retract its head into the body causing the front segments to

swell and making its eyespots prominent. The final effect is rather like a snake and the illusion is completed when the caterpillar moves the front part of its body from side to side in slow motion. The overall aim, of course, is to frighten off avian predators who might otherwise have seen the caterpillar as a tasty meal.

September
September, like March, is often a month of transition. The first leaves begin to adopt their autumnal tints and most of the flowers along the edges of rides have gone to seed. Butterflies congregate where nectar sources are still available. They are often joined by silver Y moths,

Horn of plenty

which are a migrant species to Britain and frequently active during the day as well as at night. Silver Y moths seldom settle, instead hovering in front of flowers and probing with their tongues. Where flowers fail, butterflies such as the speckled wood and comma turn to over-ripe blackberries and other fruits.

For birds and small mammals, the vast quantity of fruits and berries make this period of the year a time of great plenty.

Less welcome to the management committee is the perennial problem of rubbish being dumped in the car park, which has to be cleared up by the warden and volunteers. The haul on 27th yielded

an almost complete bathroom suite, including the proverbial kitchen sink! Quite inexcusable behaviour in these days of civic amenity sites and self-hire skips.

October
October usually proves the best time for fungi. A foray on 16th identified an impressive list of 50 species including a number of prized edible species like horn of plenty and wood blewits. A note of caution, however, to anyone attracted by the thought of food for free, Monkwood is also home to many highly poisonous species including the death cap. This is the most deadly fungus known to man and has no known antidote. A pretty convincing argument to leave fungus well alone unless positively identified by an expert.

A very special animal living at Monkwood, but one you are unlikely to see, is the dormouse. Dormice are strictly nocturnal and spend most of their time above ground level. In fact, some experts believe they are reluctant to cross open ground. Special arboreal 'mouse runs' have been provided at Monkwood to help them cross areas of coppice. The best clue to their presence is hazelnuts, a favoured food source, which are opened by the dormouse in a very distinctive manner. Unlike other small mammals, nuts opened by dormice have a smooth inner rim with the only teeth marks showing on the outer surface.

November

As the days shorten and the temperature drops, mixed parties of tits and finches are often seen moving through the wood in their quest for food. Long-tailed tits are often prominent in these flocks but perhaps the most fun to watch are the nuthatches storing nuts in tree bark crevices in preparation for the hard times ahead.

November is the month when contractors arrive to thin-out trees and cut certain coppice plots. This year the main focus is on Little Monkwood, where trees are to be thinned to promote the better specimens for future timber. Like several Trust reserves, where opportunities allow, Monkwood has to pay its way. Exploiting timber resources helps pay for other work which benefits wildlife.

Nuthatch

December

Much of the effort this winter will be in Little Monkwood where thinning and ride widening by contractors has left considerable brash on the woodland floor. This will be disposed of before next year. Regular parties of students and staff from Worcester Grammar School have proved a godsend in this work; without their efforts the clearing up would never be completed.

Piles of feathers along the edges of rides advertise the presence of sparrowhawks. Present virtually all the year, this acrobatic airborne striker can occasionally be spotted as it chases its prey through the trees.

January 1994

The first chance to put into effect all those New Year resolutions about keeping fit and losing weight came on 9th with a special woodland action day organised as part of Woolwich Action Earth, an annual campaign aimed at encouraging people to become involved in environmental activities in the immediate aftermath of Christmas.

The wood itself appears lifeless at this time of year but this is far from the case. Footprints around the pond are signs of a passing fox, while the harsh note of a hidden bird betrays the presence of jays. Another winter resident seen on 14th was the blackcap which,

Long-tailed tit

although primarily regarded as a summer visitor, is now regularly reported in southern England in winter.

February

Conservation work this month is directed to the annual task of bramble bashing. Bramble is something of a mixed blessing at Monkwood: the blossom is a favoured nectar source for many butterflies and other insects, while the fruit is greatly appreciated by many small mammals and birds; and yet, if uncontrolled, it will take over large areas smothering other plants and vegetation. It can be a particular problem within coppice plots where it suppresses the wild flowers that coppicing has been introduced to encourage. No-one on the management committee likes to see the use of chemical methods of control but, even with double the number of regular volunteers, it would be impossible to tackle this problem without them.

March

With the arrival of March, the Silver Jubilee year draws to a close and our diary of this wonderful and varied nature reserve begins a new chapter. It has been at times a hectic year, with the regular challenges of managing one of Worcestershire's premier woods being supplemented by a host of special activities and celebrations. The reward lies in the fact that Monkwood is getting better and better for wildlife, something that is obviously appreciated by the increasing numbers of visitors.

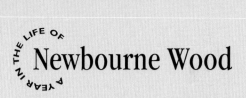
Newbourne Wood

Newbourne Wood is situated on the western side of the summit of Newbourne Hill, part of the wooded sky-line surrounding the upper Arrow valley around Alvechurch. It was formed by a glacial terminal moraine in the last ice-age between 18,000 and 14,000 years ago. The glacier had carried rocks, gravel, sand and clay with it as it drifted along. By the time it reached this area, the atmosphere was sufficiently warm for the ice to melt. The drift material was then deposited onto the underlying Keuper Marl.

Newbourne Wood is adjacent to the village of Rowney Green, near Alvechurch. Follow the public footpath which runs north-west from the road through Rowney Green at grid reference SP 045716 opposite the old post office. Turn right when you reach the wood and follow the paths in the wood. Parking is on the road side in the village.

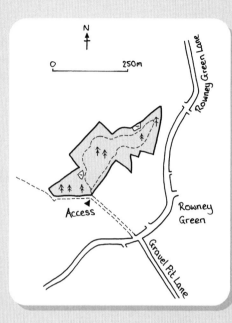

by Dorothy Snaddon

The wood lies in an area of 4½ hectares and is within the disparked twelfth century Alvechurch Park, where the Bishops of Worcester resided and hunted deer. Its boundaries comprise a small remnant of the park boundary together with old hedgerows of three closes (probably pasture) which can be still identified on a 1701 map of the park.

The reserve was given to the Trust in 1970 by Mr and Mrs Christopher Tangye, members of the Cadbury family, who lived at Rowney Lodge Farm and who had purchased the land from developers who had quarried it for sand and gravel and then 'restored' the ground. During 1958–1959 it was planted with pines, larch, chestnut, oak, beech and Douglas fir.

Since 1970 the Trust has been thinning and harvesting the conifers for timber, opening up glades and widening the rides. Plant surveys between 1970 and 1977 showed that the wood was becoming more diverse, but by 1986 the conifers had grown considerably, shading the woodland floor, so killing nearly all of the ground flora and shrub layer in the central areas.

Coal tit

Since then more conifers have been felled, bringing sunshine and green grass into the middle of the wood. Tits and goldcrest call in the canopy of the trees, chiffchaff sing on the eastern edge and lapwing sing in the surrounding fields. Recently a badger-shaped

hole was found and now a badger is gathering the surrounding grass and taking it down into its new sett for bedding.

Wild daffodil bulbs have been planted near the Dell pool. Fox Pool (a fox resides nearby) has been considerably enlarged and the surrounding alders coppiced. Clay was brought to the site and a team of volunteers came to puddle it, just like the canals were made!

The pool rapidly filled with rain water and has been planted with species from a pool at Ipsley Alders. Some tadpoles were introduced last spring and now we are awaiting the appearance of our first frog spawn.

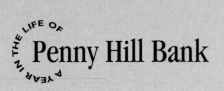
Penny Hill Bank

This small area of grassland covers less than one hectare but is sufficiently interesting to be an SSSI. It was purchased by the Trust in 1975. It lies on the east slopes of Penny Hill, north of Martley.

Restricted access to Trust members carrying membership cards. Other visitors should first apply to the Trust's office for a permit. Parking space limited on nearby roadsides.

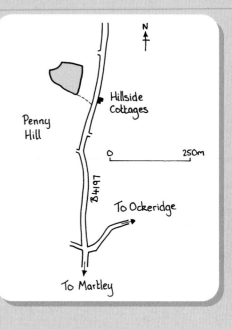

from notes by Jane and Dave Scott

The reserve is on Wenlock Silurian Limestones, which outcrop here and there in west Worcestershire. The lime-rich soil is thin and stony, and fossils, especially brachiopod shells, which have been eroded out of the rocks can be found at the surface. The ground slopes down to the east and its irregular surface indicates small-scale hand quarrying in the past.

The bank is protected by woodland and scrub to the north and west, providing shelter. The grassland is rich in flowers and about 180 species have been recorded including bee orchids, pyramidal orchids, greater butterfly-orchids, twayblade, dyer's greenweed, autumn gentian, ploughman's-spikenard, bird's-foot, rock-rose, cowslips, carline thistle and red bartsia. Several mosses uncommon in Worcestershire have been found.

Carline thistle

Although the bank faces east, it is well-protected from the north and collects plenty of sun. This, combined with the rich flora, provides rich habitats for butterflies and other insects, including grasshoppers. Butterflies include several uncommon in the county, notably wood white, brown argus, green hairstreak and dingy skipper. A considerable number of moths have been seen, including the burnet companion and lead belle moth.

The bank is one of the relatively few county sites for glow-worms and is rich in snails, which the glow-worm larvae eat.

Whitethroats breed in the nearby scrub and buzzards can be seen soaring overhead.

The site has probably been grassland for a long period, probably several hundreds of years. The steep slopes have been kept free of invading scrub by sheep grazing.

Herbicide was applied to the site in March 1974 and for the first few years in Trust ownership there were clear signs of damage, particularly the absence of gentian for several years. Since then the vegetation has fully recovered. The site is now maintained mainly by hand mowing and raking off the cut vegetation.

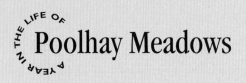

Poolhay Meadows

Three hectares of lowland meadow on the north side of the B4211 Upton upon Severn to Gloucester road at the south-west edge of Corse Lawn. The reserve comprises two adjacent SSSI meadows with a rich flora, including great burnet and meadow thistle. These are scarce plants in the county, and the presence of both of them makes this site unique in Worcestershire. There is also a ditch and old hedgerows supporting a good variety of trees and shrubs which add to the interest of the site.

At Corse Lawn on the B4211 a footpath 400 metres south of the lane to Link End runs north-west to Palmer's End Road and passes through the reserve. Open at all times but please keep to the footpath, particularly when the hay is growing. In late summer and early autumn cattle will be in the fields. Take care to close gates and to keep dogs under control.

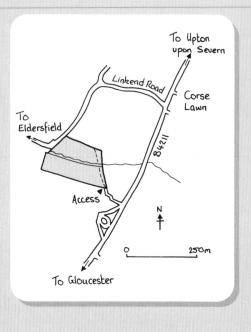

These are fairly varied lowland meadows on drained and more poorly drained neutral soils. The ditch bank with its old trees and shrubs also contains species of mosses and slugs usually found in woods, suggesting that these areas have retained a similar vegetation for a long time. The old species-rich hedges surrounding the fields add to the site's value.

The best time to visit the meadows is in May or July when the green-winged orchids and many other plants can be seen from the path.

Spring and summer

The grass and flowers grow steadily as the season advances. The two meadows are different. The northern field is wetter and supports both soft and hard rushes, cuckooflower, ragged-Robin and an abundance of green-winged orchids.

The southern meadow contains fewer orchids but there are other species of great interest. It is one of the few meadows in Worcestershire where great burnet remains abundant. This was once a common plant in flood plain meadows but has now disappeared from many sites. It is also one of the few Worcestershire sites for meadow thistle.

Great burnet

Other uncommon species include saw-wort, common spotted-orchid, pepper-saxifrage, tubular water-dropwort and adder's-tongue fern.

Although we know little of the history of the meadows the presence of these plants indicates they are old pastures and hay meadows which have not been treated with modern chemicals. The fields were attached to the Plough Inn until the Trust purchased them from West Country Brewers in 1987. Traditionally they had probably been hay meadows with aftermath grazing by horses and cattle.

After the hay is cut in July the grass is allowed to grow for a few weeks and then this aftermath is grazed by cattle until about October depending on the wetness of the season.

Autumn and winter

The fields are left for the grass and herbs to grow slowly towards the next year's hay crop.

Randan Wood

Randan Wood was the Trust's first reserve. It became a wildlife reserve in 1961 under an Agreement between the owner, Fred Fincher, and the now long-defunct West Midlands Trust. This Agreement was assigned to the present Trust in 1971, after separate county Trusts were formed to replace the West Midlands Trust. In 1988 Mr Fincher gave the wood to the Trust. Fred Fincher, now in his nineties, lived in a cottage at Randan Wood for many years. He is certainly the greatest of Worcestershire's naturalists in modern times. He was a founder member of the Trust and in the early days practically the only source of knowledge on many of the county's important wildlife sites and species. Expert on plants, insects, fungi and many other groups, his advice was often sought. Randan Wood is part of the 250 hectares of Chaddesley and other woods situated 2-3 miles north-west of Bromsgrove.

Access is restricted. To visit you must first obtain a permit from the Trust.

Great spotted woodpecker

by Fred Fincher

The reserve at Randan Wood comprises 5 hectares of woodland, roughly triangular in shape, with the apex at the northern end. Most of it is just over 120 metres above sea level with a strip of lower ground along the western side and the lowest point at the south-western corner. There is a small spring just in front of the cottage. It is on the Keuper Marl formation with a large part of the higher ground covered by glacial drift. Some of this consists of pebbles but most is a light sand. One of these pebble deposits has been removed leaving a hollow.

Wood spurge

This has become a small bog that floods in wet weather, though it lies fairly high. This adds considerably to its interest as the bog is mainly of sphagnum moss, uncommon in this area.

When I bought Randan Wood in 1933 it was in the process of being clear felled. Fortunately I arrived in time to save the best trees including the largest oaks and five fairly large yews. Most of the remaining trees were sessile oak, but with a few pedunculate oaks and some hybrid oaks. The rest were mainly ash, both downy and silver birch, and also holly, maple, gean (wild cherry), aspen, rowan, small-leaved lime and hawthorn. Hazel

was the chief shrub with some blackthorn, goat willow (or sallow), alder buckthorn, alder, guelder-rose, spindle and ivy.

Some time after my arrival I found that wild service-tree was present in many places in nearby woodland but not on my piece. I soon rectified this by planting two suckers and one of these has done very well, though still not old enough to flower. In addition I also planted some exotic species of *Sorbus*, a few conifers, two species of rhododendrons and a fly honeysuckle.

Most of the typical woodland flowers are present, including herb-Robert, wood-sorrel, primrose, wood spurge, barren strawberry, sanicle, foxglove, enchanter's-nightshade, bittersweet, angelica, marsh thistle, pignut, rough chervil,

upright hedge-parsley, lesser burdock, lesser periwinkle, daffodil, wood forget-me-not, bugle, wood sage, woodruff, nipplewort, broad-leaved willowherb, marsh cudweed, selfheal, yellow archangel, betony, three-nerved sandwort, creeping buttercup, spurge-laurel and yellow pimpernel. I have left mention to the last of two that provide the finest display: bluebell and wood anemone. Increasing shade seems to have no effect and to me they are unequalled.

A few introductions have been made. The most striking is skunk cabbage, one of the arums that likes wet ground. Then there is May lily, very rare in the wild state, but it is thriving well here and one wonders why it should be rare, marsh cinquefoil, which does well in the bog, and also solomon's-seal.

This also is a rare wild plant and not common in gardens but it provides a good example of how widely some insects range in search of their food plants. In this case the insect is a large black sawfly, *Phytoplatocira atzarima*. Only the larvae feed on the plant and they ravage it so that it seems unlikely the plant will recover but next year it comes up as good as ever. The sawfly is also said to feed on lily-of-the-valley but I have never yet seen that attacked.

A variety of butterflies is found on the reserve, of which the white admiral is probably the rarest of those seen each year.

Oak bush-cricket

There is a good list of other insects but not many can be relied on to be seen each year. The oak bush-cricket and several wood boring beetles are frequently seen. Of the latter, *Strangalia maculata*, *Rhagium mordax* and *Alosterna tabacicolor* are the most regular. This last is particularly fond of black bryony.

There is a good list of mammals but as most of these are nocturnal they are not so easy to see. Common and pygmy shrews and bank voles are frequently out in daylight, and a colony of yellow-necked mice in the cottage is well established. The muntjac is the only deer regularly present.

By March there is a good chorus of the resident birds such as song thrush, mistle thrush, robin, wren, chaffinch, great tit and bullfinch. In April they are joined by chiffchaff, willow warbler, blackcap, garden warbler and cuckoo. A few years ago nightingales were quite regular, but now one needs to go several miles further south to be sure of hearing them. Another resident, the woodcock, can be seen and heard each evening from March to August at dusk doing its roding flight. Occasionally a pied flycatcher can be seen on migration and I have had two visits by golden orioles in the past.

There are also a few sedges, of which pendulous sedge is the finest

Song thrush

but wood-sedge, thin-spiked wood-sedge and pill sedge can also be found.

Bracken and male-fern are the most common ferns but broad and narrow buckler-ferns are fairly common and lady-fern, hart's-tongue, soft and hard shield-ferns, Borrer's male-fern, lemon-scented fern, and common polypody are also present.

Other resident birds not already mentioned include all three woodpeckers, nuthatch, treecreeper and coal, blue, marsh and willow tits. The great spotted woodpecker has the habit of extracting sap from the small-leaved lime, one of the less common trees here. It bores small

holes to do this and these look like small nail holes.

Among introduced plants is monk's-hood, a plant of great interest to me as it cured me of pleurisy. At the age of 20 I had a rather bad cold which turned much worse one night. The harsh cough woke up my mother in an adjacent bedroom and finding me with a high temperature she started dosing me with homeopathic extract of this plant. The rapid action was astonishing. Several hours later the doctor arrived to diagnose an attack of pleurisy but by then I was feeling much better.

Normally this is a good area for fungi but the dryness of the last few years has much reduced the number of species. My list numbers about 500 species but many are irregular even in a good season.

Ravenshill Nature Reserve

A YEAR IN THE LIFE OF

Ravenshill Wood was originally the property of Elizabeth Barling and managed as a reserve under an Agreement with the Trust. The house and Discovery Centre are now privately owned by Colin and Sue Clark, and the 20 hectare woodland owned by the Barling family is open to visitors. The Trust sits on the reserve management committee in an advisory capacity. Ravenshill reserve was established by the late Elizabeth Barling, partly following her own innovative ideas and partly in association with the Trust. She gave a charming account of her experiences in *The Birth of a Nature Reserve*, published in 1982. The wood lies 60-120 m above sea level on sticky Keuper Marl.

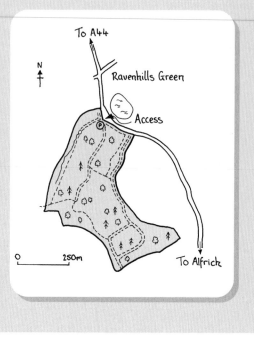

Travelling from Worcester to Bromyard on the A44, turn sharp left for Alfrick just after crossing the River Teme at Knightsford Bridge. The reserve entrance is on the right after about 1.5 miles along the Alfrick road at grid reference SO 740539. A small information centre is open from Easter to October, with toilet and picnic area. The woodland walk is open throughout the year, unless closed by the owners. Entrance is free to Trust members with membership card.

by Sue Clark

January 1993

The diary records rain, snow, wind and frost. The reserve is quiet, waiting for the spring. People come around during the day to walk their dogs and to enjoy the peace and quiet. On the odd, lovely winter day the sun goes down like a red ball, shining through the frosty trees. As you walk you can see a lot of birds, if you look carefully: nuthatches, treecreepers, green and great spotted woodpeckers, robins, thrushes, redwings and fieldfares. Towards the end of the month the miracle slowly starts to work. Dog's mercury is unbending in

Weasel

the wood and the catkins are starting to lengthen on the hazel. An occasional primrose show buds and the snowdrops nod in the wind. By the end of the month its daylight until 5 p.m., and there is something new to see almost every day.

February

One morning, as I stood drinking my coffee, I saw something running up the path. Every so often it stopped and looked all around. As it came closer I could see a white chest and hazel-brown back. The face was sharp, eyes bright and ears mobile. It stopped by the house, stood up on hind legs and had a good look about – it was a weasel. What a lovely sight!

Suddenly and quietly snow came. The bird life is fantastic. We feed them with a variety of foods so as to attract a wide range of species. The jays are very strident but their plumage against the snow is beautiful. The nuthatches land on the feeder with a very loud thump, if you are outside it is an unmistakable sound.

Walking through the unmarked snow is magical. You can see where all the animals have been and occasionally who ate who for breakfast! Towards the end of the month an occasional day of sunshine and gentle west winds blow. Is it spring?

March

Did March come in like a lion or a lamb? For once it was indecisive and the weather was quiet, cold and wet. The damp weather ensured that toads returning to their breeding pond crossed the road on their usual day, 10 March. We put out the warning signs to slow motorists down. Some ignored them but most people were very interested. The numbers crossing were not as high as in some years, but enough to ensure a healthy population in the pond. Once again, we were amazed at the diversity of colour in toads: from sulphurous yellow to almost black.

The woods are really waking from winter sleep now. The larches start to turn green and flowers start to show. Every day has something different. Violets, wood anemones, cherry blossoms and some of the early daffodils Elizabeth planted in the higher part of the wood.

As the weather improves we start to look for one of our favourite migrants and on 29 March we hear them: the chiffchaffs are back.

April

This year we had the wettest Easter Sunday we could remember. Water is running everywhere and the famous Ravenshill mud well in evidence. Very few visitors come to walk around. But, in contrast, we saw three swallows flying over the lake. They seem to meet here before going further north.

Bird activity is frantic, the air is full of song. As always the birds will find their own places to nest, anywhere but in the boxes

Wren

provided! This year a wren has built a nest in a mop head outside the back door. We move past her very quietly.

The cuckooflower comes into flower and with it come the orange-tip butterflies. The herb-Paris is growing well, every year we seem to find new clumps. It is a most unusual flower, difficult to find if you don't know it.

On St George's Day the cuckoo returned. Spring really is here now.

May

This is the time of year when insects of all sorts start to make themselves known and heard! A particular noise starts in early May and it takes a few moments for us to identify it: cockchafer beetles flying into the windows at night. If you catch them – its very easy to let them fly onto you – you can examine them. Their antennae are amazing, like two small combs, and their wing cases are very hard and a warm brown colour. As they walk over your hands their legs tickle. The noise they make when flying is very loud, like a small motor-bike.

Towards the end of the month the diary is full of moths. The poplar hawk moth is a usual sight here, and again it is the noise that gives them away. They come out at about 12.30 at night and sit by the outside lights. The moths at Ravenshill are wonderful.

Hornet

Grass snakes and slow-worms are much in evidence now, you have to be very careful where you put your feet.

June

The spotted flycatcher has finally arrived. The wet, cold weather has made it late this year. The bird, so aptly named, stays with us to raise a brood but some time during August it slips quietly away.

Whilst I was gardening I heard a 'kronk' from above. Looking up I saw five herons wheeling around then landing in the poplars. They stayed around for about 20 minutes, fighting and shouting at each other. I had a few moments imagining a heronry, just a dream I'm afraid. The last one to go sat in a tree for five minutes with its neck stretched out, pointing upwards. It looked just as if he was sun-bathing!

In the middle of the month we had several things, not very rare, but pleasing. A kingfisher sat by the pond for a few hours where he found a stick to perch on. Banded demoiselles and beautiful demoiselles were both in evidence, such lovely ephemeral insects.

July

Several hornets are around the picnic area this year. They are enormous, but very gentle. Not at all like their smaller aggressive relatives, the wasps. A very loud buzzing lets us know that the wood wasps are here. They are about two inches long with a large spike at the rear end. They are however harmless, they look much more ferocious than they are.

St Swithin's Day brought rain: it was to be prophetic.

Our new pond is settling down now and provides us with hours of entertainment. From nothing it has become a thriving ecosystem. As if from nowhere it is full of diving beetles, pond-skaters, dragonfly nymphs and numerous other larvae. But it is the dragonflies that captivate us. So many different types in all colours and sizes. This is when you realise how much you don't know.

Pond skaters

August

This is a quiet time for wildlife, but not so for visitors. The wood is busy with holiday makers of all nationalities.

Towards the end of the month, one of the most momentous times in the life of the wood begins. The poplars are to be felled having reached the end of their life. Big boughs fall off during high winds and they are now a danger.

For several weeks the sound of chain-saws echo throughout the wood and enormous lorries take the trunks away. But apart from this the wood is silent. It is as if it is holding its breath, waiting to see what happens. We are also waiting to see the effect this will have. Apart from these entries the diary is empty except for, towards the end of the month, the autumn crocuses appear. The first sign of the season changing.

September

Felling continues. What new species will we see after this, will the wood ever look clothed again?

Slowly the birds return, and then the fungi spring up everywhere. Nature is taking back her wood again. There are so many different fungi it is very difficult to decide what is what. After all the rain, the wood is very damp with good conditions for fungi.

If you get up early at this time of year, the sun shines very low through the trees which are magically festooned with spiders' webs.

October

The slow descent into winter seems to dominate the diary at this time of

year. At times warm and sunny, at times wet and windy. This year a big multi-stemmed lime tree succumbed to the wind. I was surprised by its small root ball, no wonder it blew over. Elizabeth Barling, who founded the reserve, used to find hibernating dormice in these trees, but we have never been lucky enough to see them. As the leaves fall you can see birds move clearly. Parties of long-tailed tits fly around in great numbers, they are very gregarious and 'talk' all the time.

November

This was a month of glorious colour. From the pale oaty colour of the larches to the fiery red of the American red oak. When the sun shines the birds sing their hearts out.

One evening, whilst driving along the lane, we both saw an unusual sight. A small creature low to the floor, with white rings around its eyes loped along. Could it really be a polecat? We hurried around to see if we could get closer. Yes, it was definitely a polecat.

The Worcester Conservation Volunteers usually spend a day with us in November. This year as always we are amazed by the amount of work they managed to do in such a short time. There was a lot of clearing up to do after the poplars were felled. But the WCVs make it look so easy! We are very grateful to them for all the things they have done for us over the years. These are the unsung heroes of conservation.

December

It is winter now. The frost is heavy, riming everything in white. Fog comes early and stays late, but when it clears the sky is that shade of blue you only see when the air is very clear and sharp.

Birds come in constant procession to the feeding table. We feed with the usual things, peanuts, cheese, fat, breadcrumbs, cooked rice and commercially produced birdseed. This winter we seen thrushes, chaffinches, blue, great, marsh, willow and coal tits, nuthatches, siskins, jays, green and great spotted woodpeckers. Robins also come but they wait until the table is quiet. They sing beautifully when the sun shines, a real sound of winter. On Christmas Day, I find just the tips of daffodils growing. The year turns again.

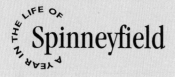
Spinneyfield

This small 1½ hectare reserve was given to the Trust by Christopher Cadbury in 1985. It lies in the hills on the Chadwich Estate about one mile east of the M5 motorway junction at Lydiate Ash, near Bromsgrove.

Restricted. All intending visitors should first contact the Trust's office for permission and to arrange access, except for visits on guided walks, usually organised in July.

Field grasshopper

by Bill Brown

Spinneyfield is a relic of the heather, gorse and scrub heathland which once covered most of the Lickey Hills. It is located on the south-west slopes of Beacon Hill with views over north Worcestershire and on to the Malverns, and over the south Shropshire hills. The best time to visit is in July. There is a pleasant walk over private land to the Heather Field with its old grassland. Here heath bedstraw, heath speedwell and milkwort can be found. The air hums with insects. Butterflies include small heath, meadow brown, ringlet,

Bladder campion

small copper, small skipper and gatekeeper, plus numerous grasshoppers and moths. Chimney-sweeper moths breed on the reserve – these are black day-flying moths with a white edge to the wing-tips.

A high stile leads on to the Gorse Field where several kinds of lichens can be found on the older gorse stems. Encroaching thorn thickets are being thinned and ash saplings coppiced to provide poles in the future. Bladder campion can be found among the gorse.

A small boggy dingle with an alder-lined stream runs down the side of the reserve.

The site slopes down quite steeply to a stream and a pond. The latter is the location of the rare shoreweed, one of its two Worcestershire sites. This scarce plant is usually found in shallow water along lake shores on sandy or gravelly somewhat acid soils. It forms tufts of half-round leaves (two facing each other to form a cylinder) and spreads with creeping and rooting runners.

The gorse and heather grow on Clent Breccia, a compacted gravel consisting of angular rock fragments in a red silt. This is overlaid in the field above with Bunter Pebble Beds. Some of the larger rounded stones that have rolled down on to the reserve are 60 cm long.

The bird-life is not exceptional. The reserve is visited by fallow deer, badger and fox.

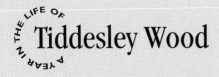

Tiddesley Wood

Tiddesley Wood lies on a low ridge above the River Avon, on heavy clay soils with small patches of gravels deposited long ago by the Avon. The wood was in monastic and church ownership for 1,300 years, first by Pershore Abbey from AD 689-1065, then Westminster Abbey from 1065-1888, and then by the Church Commissioners until purchased by the Trust in 1985.

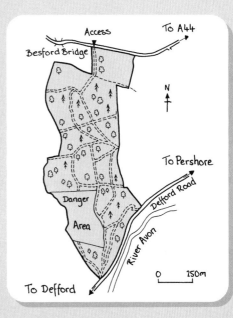

Tiddesley Wood lies about 1¼ miles west of Pershore. The main entrance is west of Allesborough Hill Farm at the north end of the wood, grid reference SO 929461, on the minor road from Pershore to Besford Bridge and Croome. Park by the road side (off-road parking should be available soon). A gated track leads to the wood. Please take care not to block the entrance. The reserve is open at all times apart from Christmas Day. It is essential that you keep your dog under control in this wood. There is a military firing range and danger area situated at the south-west corner of the wood. Red flags are hoisted when the range is in use– do not pass them. Visitors must not enter the fenced area behind the butts at any time. During forestry operations timber is often piled along the rides. Do not let children climb on the stacks, which may fall and cause injury. Note that the extreme north-east corner of the wood (about 5½ hectares) is privately owned and not open to visitors.

---

by Bert Reid

Friday 30 April 1993

The main event of the year in the wood is the open day, held during Worcestershire Wildlife Week in May, and for months my colleagues on the local committee have been busy with booking exhibitors, organising publicity, planning refreshments, refurbishing stalls and many, many other tasks. My job is to look after the money and to lead some guided walks on the day.

This evening I pay a visit to the wood to plan my route for the walks and to keep an eye open for any problems we may encounter on the big day.

Bugle

Taking the path up to the bridleway, I see that the herb-Paris is flowering well and notice a few adder's-tongue ferns. By the memorial seat a fine patch of ramsons is in full flower. The bluebells will be just past their best for the open day but will still make a good show.

Along the bridleway the bugle is in flower but the wood anemones are almost finished and we will only see a very few isolated flowers on the day. The ragged-Robin is a long way from flowering and the aspen seeds are not yet well developed. At last year's open day the aspen was just shedding its cotton wool seeds, leaving the path covered in white as

though with snow. I think that this year we will be too early for a repeat performance.

Sunday 9 May

Open day in the wood: I drag myself unwillingly out of bed at 7 a.m. still stiff and tired from yesterday's preparation – loading, unloading, shifting, building, leafleting etc. Arrive at the wood by eight to find a dull day with a strong cold wind. The marquee and stalls have all survived the overnight weather so I start work with some final tidying up of tables, chairs and so on.

By now the first exhibitors are arriving so all hands set to helping them unload so that we can turn the vehicles round quickly. This is the time of greatest chaos with helpers rushing in all directions, unwilling animals being persuaded to go into

their pens rather than eating the wood, and cars and lorries seemingly in total gridlock.

9.30 a.m. and I now have an excuse to take a rest from physical labour since it is time for me to distribute the cash floats to the Trust stalls.

10 a.m. and we open to the public. I am now off duty until my first guided walk at 11 a.m. so I take the opportunity to check out my planned route through the wood. I am delighted to find my first bird's-nest orchid of the year in a place where I can easily show it to our visitors.

By 11 a.m. it is still cold and dull, and the car park field is far from full. I set out with my first group. A brief history of the wood, a look at the variety of trees, explain coppice management, admire the herb-Paris,

confuse them with the hawthorn hybrids, on past the ramsons and bird's-nest orchid, up to the early-purple orchids, down the bridle path looking at aspen, bugle and various sedges, past the pear trees, discuss the ferns, then the rain starts. Get steadily wetter as we see the fragrant agrimony and the meadow saffron. Then finally back to the start.

The afternoon goes in a blur. Three guided walks with no break between and my feet are aching and my voice is getting hoarse. The weather redeems itself at last and crowds arrive. By the time I have finished it is 5 p.m. and the open day is over.

The aftermath of the day is like a film run backwards. I gather in the money, pay out expenses, and drive home to get the takings to a place of safety. Then straight back to the

wood to help with taking down the marquee, removing the stall covers, and loading up tables, chairs, artist screens, hurdles etc. on to vehicles. Then drive over to Lower Smite Farm for the unloading and storing in the barns ready for the next event.

Arrive home at 8.30 p.m. but still not finished, I have the money to count, bag and record. Sorting, adding and checking can't be rushed but eventually all is complete and the Trust has made a little over £2,000, so the hard work was worth it.

11 p.m. and all is well, just time for a good soak in a hot bath before collapsing into bed at the end of an exhausting but worthwhile day.

Saturday 26 June

Today is my first chance to visit the wood since a holiday in Ireland so I expect to see a few changes. Near

the entrance a few plants of grey field-speedwell are growing – this is only occasionally found in the wood and grows in more disturbed spots. The white-legged damselflies are all around today. These breed commonly on the Bow Brook which runs by the wood and many come into the wood after emergence to feed up before returning to the water to mate.

By the main ride the yellow-wort is in flower. This is one of my favourite plants with yellow starry flowers contrasting with the grey-green leaves which are joined in pairs so the stem runs through the middle. The water figworts are also out and I manage to find some of the figwort weevils well-camouflaged on the flower heads. The sinister looking scorpion fly is nearby, sitting on a hazel leaf with its tail curved up like a real scorpion.

As it gets dark I go to see if there are any glow-worms about. The wood has had a small colony of glow-worms along the main ride and the bridlepath for a long time, but it is unusual to see more than four or five on any evening. As the light fades I soon see the first cold green pin-point of light as the wingless female beetle signals to flying males.

As I walk on I see another, then a small group, then more. In total I manage to find 25 glow-worms including one male, which has a much reduced glow but which resembles a normal beetle, unlike the worm-like female. This is an excellent end to the evening. I have never before seen more than about ten in one night.

Saturday 24 July

July is the peak month for butterflies in the wood, both in number of species and individuals. On a few memorable occasions I have seen more than 20 species in a day, but butterfly numbers are low this year and we will be lucky to find more than a dozen or so.

A favourite feeding place for many of our butterflies is on the teasel heads and it is always worth a good look here. Peacock butterflies are especially fond of the teasels. This species is widespread and common and we tend to ignore it but is it one of our most attractive insects, with a complex mix of colours – red, blue, yellow, white and black. If it were rare, naturalists would make special trips to find it, but luckily it can be admired in almost any garden with a buddleia bush. Also on teasel I see a painted lady butterfly, an immigrant which is scarce this year.

My own favourite butterfly is the white admiral. It glides gracefully in the sunshine, dances in the breeze and soars majestically to the tree tops. It is very variable in numbers – in the best years I have seen twenty or more in a day but numbers have been very low for the last two or three years. Such fluctuations are often found in butterflies which have very exact habitat requirements and are very dependent on weather conditions. A couple of weeks earlier I had watched half a dozen females flying along the ride seeking the perfect honeysuckle plants in the shade on which to lay their eggs, so I had been hopeful that we would see some today. At last we find them. First a good look at one resting in the sunshine on an elm leaf and then a second flitting along the ride.

Saturday 7 August

Five or six years ago I took a party of naturalists from near Northampton around the wood. They enjoyed the visit so much that a group of them have visited each summer since, and this year one of their number phoned to ask where they could find violet helleborines in the wood since they had not managed to find them on earlier visits. Since I was free I said that I would join them in the wood and show them the plants.

We then set off straight away for the closest patch of violet helleborine. This interesting plant is a member of the orchid family and closely related to the commoner broad-leaved helleborine, but with leaves of a curious grey-green colour, tinged

Meadow saffron

with violet. Its flowers are a rather dingy white with pale green sepals flushed with purple. It is easily overlooked since it seems to blend into the background and often grows in quite dense shade. On rare occasions a violet helleborine will appear without any green chlorophyll. Such a plant has been seen next to the others for a number of years now. This variety looks quite different. Without any green coloration, the whole plant is a striking violet colour and poses a real problem of identification to anyone who relies on normal books.

Sunday 12 September

Today I go to look particularly at one special ride. Here, some of our late flowering plants are found, attracting insects to them for a last feed of nectar for the year. A good patch of meadow saffron grows here. This crocus-like plant is sometimes called naked ladies because its beautiful flowers appear in the autumn bare of any leaves. On a thin whitish flower stalk the pale purple cups open wide to provide a fine show at this time of year. The leaves will not be seen until next spring when they come up with the bluebells, the fruit from this years flowers nestling at the base of the leaf rosette. I think that this is our only native plant which flowers one year but sets its seeds the next. This patch of meadow saffron has stayed within the same boundaries for many years, neither spreading nor reducing. We

also have another good patch, this time well away from any rides, and a few scattered plants elsewhere.

The fragrant agrimony grows along the same ride. This looks like a larger and bushier common agrimony with similar yellow flowers and leaf shape. The books tell you that the fragrant agrimony can be distinguished by the reflexed outermost bristles on the fruit, but there is an easier way. Lightly press a leaf and sniff. The fragrance referred to in the common name is not the smell of the flowers but is the scent held in tiny glands on the leaves. A little rub on a leaf releases the scent which is delightful, the equal of many expensive perfumes. The fragrant agrimony is a rare plant in Worcestershire and the wood is one of its main strong-holds.

The third late-flowering plant on the ride is the devils'-bit scabious. This gets its name from its short truncated tap-root looking as though it has been bitten off. The flower head has many small blue florets held on a tall stem, and some of the flowers linger very late in the year. The flower has easily accessible nectar and pollen and is very attractive to insects at a time when few other flowers are available. Bees, beetles, hoverflies and butterflies are all here today to join in the feast.

Sunday 17 October

The autumn is here and the leaves are starting to fall. The autumn colours give the wood a completely different appearance. One of the great attractions of woodland is the way that the seasons are so clearly marked: the wood changes from the bareness of winter, through the pale

Fragrant agrimony

greens of spring, the many colours of summer to the browns and yellows of autumn.

The first thing to catch my eye is a patch of shaggy ink-caps growing in the parking area. This persuades me that it is time to suffer the annual frustration of trying to identify some of the fungi growing in the wood. The shaggy ink-cap is very distinctive, starting off buffish white and gradually opening and blackening around the edge until finally it turns into a liquid sludge of black spores. Its appearance in its early stages has given it the alternative name of lawyer's wig.

I am briefly puzzled by hundreds of small pale disks lying on the ride. Closer inspection shows them to be spangle galls, which have fallen off the oak leaves overhead. This gall is caused by a tiny gall wasp that lays its eggs on the oak leaves, which respond by forming the disk of plant material enclosing the egg. The developing larva feed on the gall material and in September the galls fall to the ground. They over-winter here covered by the fallen leaves. In April the next generation hatch but this time lay their eggs on the catkins, forming currant galls. When these hatch out the adults mate and repeat the cycle by returning to the leaves for egg-laying. The oak leaf spangle gall is often extremely common with 20 or more galls on most leaves on the trees.

Sunday 14 November

Approaching the wood by the orchard I notice that the flocks of redwings and fieldfares are back – a sure sign that summer is at an end. Recent winds and rain have stripped most of the trees bare of their leaves and the wood has a sombre look despite the first sunshine for some days.

Leafy liverwort

Although the trees are bare and the flowers are finished there is still some green to see. The ferns are more obvious now and this is a good time to hunt them out. Male-fern and broad buckler-fern are the commonest ferns in the wood and these are easily found. The soft shield-fern is next, then on to one of the few patches of bracken. Here I look for the narrow buckler-fern at a spot where I have found it in the past but without success today.

The mosses and liverworts show up well at this time of year. My favourite is the feather moss *Thuidium tamariscinum*. This has much divided leaves and sprawls over wide areas under the trees. A very beautiful plant. A rather upright bushy moss with red stem growing nearby carries the name *Rhytidiadelphus triquetrus*. Most of the leafy liverworts, which look like mosses at first glance, are small and inconspicuous but I manage to find one of the larger species *Plagiochila asplenioides*.

Sunday 19 December

This is the dead time of year in the wood. The trees are bare, the flowers are a distant memory and the birds are silent. A sombre pause while the wood rests, awaiting the first stirrings of spring and a new season. Even a contemplative walk is difficult with boots sticking obstinately in the mud. A more active approach is needed to hunt out points of natural history interest.

Many small invertebrates are still around but are hidden away in shelter. Turning over a dead log under the trees I find that there is life even at this time. Millipedes and slugs of all shapes, sizes and colours abound. Large black slugs are very common, as are smaller whitish ones and I find a handsome spotted slug under one large log. These slugs play a vital role in breaking down dead leaves and recycling the nutrients. Snails of many species are also here – small round flat ones, larger globular ones; and the narrowly conical spirals of the door snails.

Saturday 15 January 1994

By the car park, a few hopeful robins, great tits and blue tits are already thinking of attracting mates and are in full song. The great tit's incessant 'teacher teacher' call is particularly noticeable, contrasting with the thin melody of the robin and the cheerful trill of the blue tit.

A blackbird soon joins in with its alto fluting.

Blue tit

A jay calls harshly from the trees and flies over the ride. On to a side ride through the conifers I see the piles of cones stripped by the grey squirrels feeding on the seeds.

These attractive rodents are unfortunately a serious pest in woodlands, causing much damages to the timber crop. On occasions I have seen quite large trees killed by squirrels stripping off much of the bark, and many other trees are damaged by having their leading

shoots nibbled, causing branching on the main trunk.

In the conifers large flocks of tits are feeding. Blue tits, great tits and coal tits are joined by the tiny goldcrests in a ceaseless search for food. Every nook and cranny is investigated for spiders, insects or anything else edible and the air is full of the little contact calls that keep the flock together. Then suddenly the flock move away leaving silence.

Back through the conifers I spot another party of goldcrests and a treecreeper. This small mouse-like bird spirals upwards around a tree trunk searching for food, then flies down from high on one tree to the lower trunk of another. The treecreeper is a surprisingly scarce winter visitor to the wood and seems to be absent in the summer.

Finally I watch closely a mixed flock of goldcrests, redpolls and long-tailed tits all investigating the dead heads of great willowherb until they too sense my presence and move away. A solitary crow flies over followed shortly by a party of wood pigeons heading towards the orchard. All in all an excellent visit at a time when the wood can be rather uninteresting.

Sunday 27 February

Throughout the winter we hold volunteer work parties on the last Sunday of each month. My normal job is rather desk-bound so I welcome the chance to work up an honest sweat with physical labour, even though my muscles complain at the unaccustomed exercise.

Rabbits abound in the wood and this has given us a problem with a neighbouring farmer whose crops were being eaten. A few years ago therefore we erected a rabbit proof fence along the critical part of our boundary. Since then the vegetation has grown up around the fence and our task for the day is to clear away the brambles from the fence to maintain it as an effective barrier.

We don our thorn-proof gloves and get to work with slashers, being careful not to hit the fence or each other, or else simply grab the bramble stems and pull as hard as we can.

I set to with great gusto and soon have a good pile of uprooted bramble behind me. Half an hour later I am still pulling but not quite so quickly, and by the time an hour has passed by back and arms are aching and I am ready for a rest. Another group has been gathering brushwood from a recently cleared coppice plot so I

walk over to see how they are getting on, hoping no-one will notice me slacking.

I am pleased to see that the fire is blazing well. We will get our baked potatoes for lunch!

Saturday 26 and Sunday 27 March

A few years ago contractors working in the wood thinned some conifers and converted the thinnings to posts. This involved stripping the bark off and sharpening the ends with a machine like a giant pencil sharpener. After the work had been completed we were left with a large and rather unsightly pile of mixed bark and wood shavings.

By the autumn of 1993 the material in the pile was quite well rotted down and one of my colleagues had the idea of offering it for sale to the public for use as a garden mulch etc. To our surprise, we sold nearly £400 worth and immediately decided to try again in early spring.

We purchased some more bags and advertised the chippings for sale in the wood on the mornings of the 26 and 27 March. On the Saturday our opening time was 10 a.m., so just after 9 a.m. a group of us assembled with bags and shovels to get a small stock ready bagged for sale.

We should have started earlier. One of our first customers wanted 100 bags – we could not cope and so offered him 50 now and 50 tomorrow. By the time the first half of his order was complete customers had filled the car park and were getting impatient. We frantically kept on filling the bags but every time we looked like getting on top the job another customer would arrive wanting 20 or 30 bags instead of the ones and twos we had expected.

We had more helpers on the Sunday so coped rather better but still the crowds kept coming. At last the morning finished and we shut up shop. We had turned our mountain of chippings into a molehill and had earned the Trust another £1,300, a result beyond our most optimistic imaginings.

That afternoon, taking a relaxing walk, I found the first early cowslip flowers starting to open; it is for such natural beauty that so many people are prepared to give their time and effort. The funds raised by the weekend's work will help just a little to ensure that the plants and wildlife of our beautiful county can continue to be enjoyed by us and those who follow us.

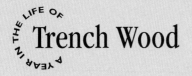

Trench Wood

Trench Wood lies on fairly level ground at the top of a south-west facing scarp slope. It is on Lower Lias clayey basic soils. The Trust owns about 43 hectares of the 62 hectare wood. This is an ancient woodland site; historically a coppice-with-standards oak wood it was cleared in the early 1960s and used to produce fast-growing whitewood poles for brush-handle making. Following purchase by the Trust in 1986 the wood is managed partly as high forest and partly as scrub or coppice. Purchase of the wood was assisted by Butterfly Conservation, who also play an active part in managing the reserve.

The wood is in the parish of Huddington at Sale Green about 2 miles north-east of junction 6 (Warndon) on the M5 motorway. Entrance is from Trench Lane, the road from Dunhampstead to Huddington, which flanks the north-east side of the road, at grid reference SO 930589. Just within this entrance turn right into a small car park. Note that the areas of woodland with big mature trees in the south-east and north-west are not part of the reserve and are not open to visitors. It is essential that you keep your dog under control in this wood.

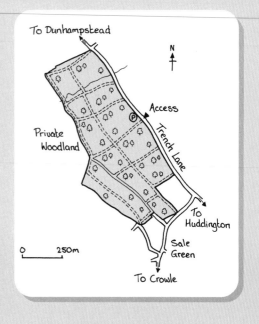

by Ken Thomas

Late March 1993

The first chiffchaffs have arrived and redpolls are still present in numbers. The wood ants' nests at the north end of the wood are already active and the bees in the hole in the old oak are showing well on warm days. Comma, small tortoiseshell and peacock butterflies have been seen. Wood anemones and wood-sorrel are out and the first bluebells has been seen. Early dog-violets and primroses are well in flower. The scarlet elf-cup fungus found on the stream at the north end of the wood is still showing but is going over. Buzzard seen on 29th, there have been several sightings recently. The last volunteer work party of the year included the erection of four bench-seats at strategic parts of the wood.

April

On the 2nd a nuthatch was seen 'plastering' a nest-hole. By the 4th several chiffchaffs were singing and the butterfly transect recording has begun for the 7th season. Second week sees heavy rain with pools everywhere; by now at least five willow warblers have joined the chiffchaffs and a blackcap has been heard. Curlew present both to the west and east of the wood can be heard on many occasions. Early season peacock numbers are peaking at 34. Leaves of twayblade and meadow saffron can be seen. Bee flies are around and goldilocks buttercups are flowering. By the middle of the month peacock numbers are declining but brimstones increasing. The first speckled wood seen. Willow warblers now outnumber chiffchaffs. The first nightingale heard on the 24th in the section of Trench known as Pope's wood. A garden warbler also heard. By the last week two nightingales were present and flowers include herb-Paris, bugle and early-purple orchid. The

Nightingale

wild garlic (ramsons) is becoming very obvious to the senses! On the 28th a female hobby was reported.

May

Muntjac sighted early in the month (they can be seen at any time in the year). Worcestershire Wildlife Week sees the now annual evening public guided walks to hear nightingales. Neither the weather nor the three singing birds were very cooperative, but most of the many people who attended the three evenings heard at least one songster. There appear to be no grasshopper warblers this year and no woodcocks roded for visitors, but tawny owl calls seemed to surround the wood. Arrow Valley Countryside group shown around on 13th – they were able to hear two nightingales.

Tawny owl

By the middle of the month many more flowers are in evidence: tormentil, wild strawberry, wood spurge, bitter-vetch, twayblade, cuckooflower and several adder's-tongue fern are found. The first small and green-veined white butterflies appear. We awaited hopefully for the offspring of the marsh fritillary butterflies introduced last year to emerge and we were relieved to find up to 20 basking in the sun on 29th. Three grizzled skippers were also present and drinker moth caterpillars found in three places. A longhorn moth found the next day; spotted-orchids and wood avens in

Foxglove

flower. Foxgloves in flower at main entrance.

June

In the first week of the month greater butterfly-orchids were in flower in several places and guelder-rose also. Cuckoos occasionally heard and the first large skipper butterflies were seen. Broad-bodied chaser dragonflies were around and also scorpionflies. The first white admiral was noted on 21st, the prelude to an exceptional season. On the same date over 40 long-tailed tits were seen: obviously a good breeding season.

By the end of the month numbers of white admirals seen on a walk easily exceeded 40. The first ringlets appeared and a banded demoiselle. Most flowers under the woodland canopy are now over but enchanter's-nightshade, wood avens, herb-Robert and bittersweet occur in areas of semi-shade. On the damper rides the marsh thistles have stems over 2 m in height, and they are accompanied by ragged-Robin, rosebay willowherb, spearwort and figwort.

Greater burnet-saxifrage

A wealth of flowers begin to bloom on the open sunny rides including the devils'-bit scabious essential for the marsh fritillary caterpillars. A red admiral occurred on several days and on 26th a nightingale was

carrying food. White-letter hairstreak reported and buzzard frequent. A white-legged damselfly at the end of the month.

July

The early part of the month produced a good variety of moths including drinker, clouded border, and the day-flying five-spot burnet. Dragonflies included southern hawker and common darter. With the impressive numbers of white admiral it was not unexpected to find a specimen of the variety which is almost all black. Ringlets on the transect peaked at 116 and a few commas were seen together with the first gatekeepers and meadow browns.

Dull weather persisted for much of the second half of the month but the first small skippers emerged and the only holly blue of the year was recorded. Both grass snakes and slow-worms are around. Both white-letter and purple hairstreak are flying: the two species can be confused when they are around the tree tops.

On the grassy rides bird's-foot-trefoil, betony, hedge bedstraw and tormentil are typical colourful plants. Many other species occur such as centaury, saw-wort (much favoured by gatekeepers), greater knapweed, and wood sage. On the damper rides valerian, corn mint, water-pepper seen together with the local speciality greater burnet-saxifrage. On the west edge of the wood are plants not found elsewhere, such as wild basil and musk mallow.

August

During the month butterfly totals are at their greatest, often over 200 individuals being recorded on the transect alone. Autumn brimstones build to their peak, as do gatekeepers and peacocks. Small skipper numbers are high at the start of the month; white admiral, large skipper and ringlet are tailing off. It is rather quiet for bird-life, although some willow warblers and chiffchaffs sing. All three woodpeckers can be seen at times. Buzzards, kestrels, and sparrowhawks have been seen intermittently.

Plants at their best on the rides include teasel, burdock (good for peacocks), and rosebay willowherb. Colourful berries are forming on honeysuckle, alder buckthorn, guelder-rose and dogwood.

Meadow saffron, one of the reserve's specialities, flowers towards the middle of the month, and a patch on one of the rides has been cleared to enable the flowers to show in good light; the colour is much brighter than on plants flowering in heavily shaded places.

September

Flocks of tits can be found including blue, great, marsh, coal and long-tailed and, as the autumn advances, treecreepers, chaffinches and goldcrests may be associated with the tits. The start of the month saw a few of the impressive elephant hawk moth caterpillars on rosebay willowherb. A few autumn commas are emerging. There is one very large hornbeam on the west edge of the reserve; this year it has dropped copious amounts of seed.

The wood contains a good range of fungi which are at their best now.

October

Thoughts turn to maintenance and improvements. Work parties are held every month through to March with variable levels of support from Trust and Butterfly Conservation members. This year the initial work was concentrated on scrub clearance as previous years' emphasis on ride widening had prevented this. A block was cleared with the help of Worcester Conservation Volunteers. The Trust staff did the annual mowing of rides and open areas.

November

The Trust work party continued the October project and Butterfly Conservation members cleared

encroaching scrub from one of the main rides.

Redpoll numbers are building up (over 80 seen on 16th) and smaller numbers of siskin are calling. The occasional woodcock seen.

December

Work parties continued and contractors began thinning three large blocks of timber. The timber is not of a large enough size to be used for other than the pulp market. The contractors also widened another ride. Goldcrests are abundant this year, especially in Pope's Wood.

January 1994

Contractors had to stop extracting timber due to the wet conditions. Early primroses flowering towards the end of the month.

February

Trust work parties concentrated their efforts on clearing the brash left by contractors on the main ride. The Trust had three more entrances stoned and three new wooden gates erected on Trench Lane (one of the gates was stolen soon afterwards, and a new metal gate had to be provided). The use of the boxes on the notice-board for a recording book and a place for information leaflets has been stopped because of continual vandalism.

Woodcock seen occasionally. Foxes and stoats seen. Dog's mercury well in flower and

Woodcock

bluebells shoots showing. The various sallows flower early.

March

All winter work completed and remainder of timber extracted. Hazel whips planted in recently cleared block. In an effort to increase the range of habitat in the wood a start has been made on clearing an area where a pond can be dug. Curlews well established near the wood and a heron flew over on 6th. Chiffchaffs were back by the 20th. Brimstone and peacocks seen on 24th, buzzards seen on many days. Willow tit singing on 25th. Comma on 29th.

Tunnel Hill Meadow

This 1 hectare reserve near the Lenches is on gently sloping land bordered by broad-leaved woodland on three sides. It lies on the edge of a ridge of Lower Liassic limestones overlooking the Avon valley.

Access is restricted. The land is owned by the BBC and it is essential that intending visitors first contact either the Trust's office or the warden so that the necessary arrangements can be made.

Meadow brown

---

by Arthur Cundall

Tunnel Hill Meadow is not a meadow, it may never have been and certainly not in the 21 years that it has been under Trust management. Rarely visited, except by the unauthorised and by the monthly work or survey parties, it is a secluded grassy place nearly surrounded by woods, with a wide diversity of plants and insects. From its state in 1972, when invading scrub from the surrounding woodland threatened its existence, it has changed to a well-managed grassland reserve. Based on limy soils it contains several uncommon plants and butterflies are abundant.

January and February 1993

These winter months saw considerable progress in removing the regenerating bramble and dogwood that bordered the western wood. Always a borderland zone, but full of teasel and St John's-wort, and where several plants of gromwell occur in July the invading scrub has to be regularly cut back to keep the ground open for the flowers. Birds are rarely seen in winter, although the thin calls of distant parties of tits foraging in the woods could occasionally be heard. As we finished work in the February dusk a vixen's screams from close by set our nerves tingling.

Hairy violet

March and April

Sunshine for the work day and a plague of small flies which, through their close attention to eyes, ears and nose, made work in the open grassland too uncomfortable for pleasure. A blackcap in excited song passed through and a buzzard circled over the surrounding woods. The latter were still evident in April. Buzzards are becoming more frequent in the hilly and wooded areas of central and east Worcestershire, benefiting from the abundance of rabbit prey and the relative scarcity of gamekeepers. The grassland, from an apparently lifeless state, was showing the flowers of hairy violet and primroses. On the edges of the surrounding woodland wayfaring trees were flowering and a solitary seedling found in the centre of the reserve was marked for careful transplanting in the autumn to a place where it would be more welcome.

May and June

Late in May the grassland was showing its mid-summer promise, but little was really flowering and it was not until June that the orchids were at their best: spotted-orchids, twayblades and bee orchids all grow on the reserve and wasp variant of the bee orchid can be seen in a nearby field. A butterfly that excited us most apparently showed the characteristics of a wood white, but the small element of doubt that still exists over the occurrence precludes a firm claim of a new record. Other grassland butterflies showed in good numbers. Clouds of marbled whites, small blues and small coppers, together with gatekeepers and meadow browns, were among the species seen. Early in the season a holly blue or two were on the wing.

Marbled white

July

A botanical survey in July gave 100 flowering plants and grasses. Following on from work in earlier years the survey of invertebrates continued and the total number of species of all orders reached a modest 88. These records include two rare beetles, qualifying for Red Data Book status on a national basis, so the reserve continued to justify its existence.

As part of a programme to better understand the reserve and its management two study plots were set out on the grassland and surveyed in July. Taking the form of 10 × 10 metre squares it was agreed that one plot should be cut annually, to assess botanical changes resulting from this form of grassland management in comparison with an adjacent uncut plot.

August

In the course of another search for invertebrates an immature common lizard was seen, demonstrating the continued existence of this rare reptile on the reserve: it has occasionally been seen in the past. Another sighting was made at the end of October. August, however is the month when the autumn gentian is in flower, and a good widespread distribution was found this year.

Common lizard

September

With the woolly thistles in seed it was a time to walk round and plan winter activities. The seedlings of ash, thorn, rose and bramble prominent in the grassland were noted. Most would be removed in the winter when the wet soil permitted easy weeding.

October

Daylight and good weather allowed the first work day to continue until 6.30 p.m. A few of the tall ash trees, which were a potential shade problem, were felled and three were set aside for ring barking to provide dead standing timber for the insect world.

Autumn gentian

November

A day, redolent of autumn at its best, saw the 10 × 10 metre square cut, the grass being taken to the adjacent badger sett for use as bedding. We hope the badgers appreciated our thoughtfulness. Both the weeding programme and coppicing in the adjacent woodland belt began in earnest. The annual task of weeding out invading scrub from the grassland is necessary to prevent the meadow becoming scrubland and eventually woodland. Work days would continue through the winter, as they have in the past.

Not an exciting year. But Tunnel Hill is not a place for excitement. It is a peaceful reserve full of life, if closely studied. Spiders, butterflies, beetles, the occasional dragonfly, the flowers and grasses. A compact, unique patch of grassland tucked away amongst big woods.

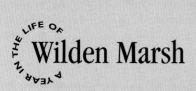
Wilden Marsh

Wilden Marsh lies just south of Kidderminster between Wilden Lane and the River Stour. It is an extensive area of dry and marshy fields with small alder and willow woods and many drainage ditches. There are old settling pits used to contain sugar-beet washings from the nearby British Sugar Corporation factory.

The marsh is just south of Kidderminster off Wilden Lane. Wilden Lane is a very busy road with few parking spaces: take care. There are gated entrances off the Lane at grid references SO 825730 and SO 829735, which lead to parts of the reserve open at all times. Visitors to the more northerly part of the reserve should obtain a permit from the Trust's office. This reserve is complex and new visitors should consult a map. Cattle will be on the reserve at times so ensure that all gates are secured after use. Parts of this reserve are dangerous, with boggy areas, steep banks by the River Stour and deep ditches.

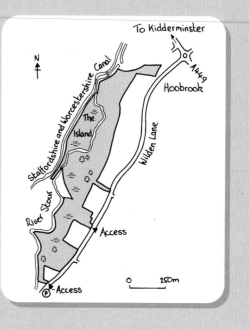

by Nigel Davies and Roger Robinson

A reserve with many different facets, Wilden changes from year to year depending on the rainfall. It consists of grazing meadows, alder carr, reed beds, and the British Sugar Corporation lagoons, all with different flora and fauna.

Much of the interest in Wilden stems from the variety of passage migrants and resident birds which may be found there, making it one of the most important wetland areas in the county.

The marsh is also of considerable value botanically. The area around the lagoons is subject to earth-moving at times,

Willow pollard

and hence provides a totally different habitat.

This is a reserve with a high management requirement. The meadows need grazing, and thus a lot of fencing work is necessary, particularly as the wet ground soon rots the posts. There are many willow trees bordering the ditches, which have to be pollarded on a regular basis. And every year a depressing amount of Himalayan balsam appears. This introduced plant is the scourge of many damp areas. It has to be uprooted and hung over a tree or fence to dry out, otherwise it will re-root. Goats are excellent at scrub and balsam control, but at present there are none in the neighbourhood.

January 1993

Siskins usually seen in their largest numbers. Early speedwells appear, especially around the lagoons.

February

The pollarding season – provided that the willows in question are not too waterlogged. Volunteers have a marked reluctance to help a chainsaw operator who is dropping heavy branches into several inches of not entirely fresh floodwater.

March

Marsh-marigolds appear as the floodwater begins to drop. Chiffchaffs and sand martins arrive, an early sign of spring approaching.

April

A busy month. Volunteers check fences and access points in

preparation for the summer grazing. Cuckooflower attracts orange-tip butterflies to the meadows. Birders eagerly look for signs of breeding little-ringed plover and redshank. Passage waders, wheatears, and the first hobbies of the year find their way into the record book at the entrance to the lagoon area. The local team start counting the various warblers.

May

As the floodwater recedes further, southern marsh-orchids flower, together with ragged-Robin and yellow iris. Garden warblers can be heard by those able to identify their song.

June

Marsh cinquefoil can be found in flower in most years. Meadowsweet dominates many areas. Himalayan balsam flowers appear to taunt volunteers who only planned a quick stroll before lunch.

July

All the summer grazing areas are needed to keep the cattle fed. Lapwings begin to gather into post-breeding flocks.

August

Balsam-pulling becomes the order of the day: a never-ending task that, on hot days, the mosquitoes and clegs can make unpleasant.

September

An unpredictable month: some years there is very little to see, in others rare vagrant birds make it one of the highlights.

Marsh cinquefoil

October

Passage migrant birds reach their highest numbers of the autumn.

November

The remaining cattle are taken off to their winter quarters. Redwings and fieldfares begin to appear. Pollarding and other woodland and scrub management begins again.

December

Winter migrants reach their highest numbers. The thinning vegetation makes it easier to flush common and Jack snipe. Occasionally a fox may be seen tip-toeing over the ice, or the weird call of a water rail may be heard from a flooded carr.

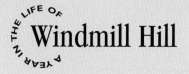

Windmill Hill

Windmill Hill is a 6 hectare grassland and scrubland reserve. It is part of the north-south escarpment which stretches from Marlcliff to Blackminster and faces west over the valley of the River Avon. The geology is interesting as the Rhaetic beds are well-represented. Above the bridleway the hill is capped with Lower Lias limestones and below them is a twenty foot band of Rhaetic clays and shales, the bottom marked by the path through the middle of the reserve. The steeper slope below the Rhaetic is Mercian mudstone. The soils are generally basic and limy and support a rich community of wildlife.

The entrance to the reserve is on the south side of the B4510, the Evesham (Bengeworth) to Littletons road, at grid reference SP 072477, approximately 800 m from the Fish and Anchor Inn and just before the brow of the hill. Cars can be parked at the roadside opposite the entrance, but please take care as the road is quite busy with poor visibility for approaching traffic. The public bridleway borders the east side of the reserve at the top of the hill and visitors may also use other paths. Please use the stiles and always shut gates as sheep are grazed on the reserve from time to time. Dogs must be kept under control at all times.

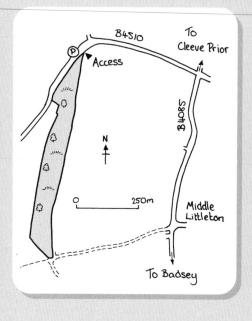

by Terry Knight

Over the last four hundred years or more the escarpment has been rough grazing land with some scrub and woodland. During this century, because of changing agricultural practices, neglect and other reasons, scrub and woodland have come to predominate and, apart from Windmill Hill, nearly all remaining grassland has been ecologically damaged by chemicals, or destroyed by market gardening or ploughing. To conserve the kilometre length of ecologically undamaged Rhaetic grassland at Windmill Hill and its associated flora and fauna, developed over a

Cow parsley

thousand years or so, the site was declared an SSSI in 1975.

The Trust bought Windmill Hill in 1979 and have since reintroduced traditional management by erecting fences to enclose sheep to graze the grassland, and by cutting back the edges of invading scrub.

The monthly walks start from the reserve's entrance on the B4510 at the top of "Fish and Anchor" bank. At the top of the entrance bank the route bears right and leads to a stile into the first enclosure. From here the path is mostly on the level, through the middle of each of the five fenced enclosures, and then

bears uphill to meet the bridleway. The return route is along the bridleway back to the road.

The hillside is uneven under the grass, and in dry weather the grass becomes very slippery on the slopes. You are strongly advised not to wander off the recognised paths, and take care, particularly in wet weather when they too become slippery with mud.

Sunday 18 April 1993

A windy and cloudy afternoon. The cow parsley by the entrance is flowering and trails of dry grass show that badgers have been renewing their bedding. On the way to the stile into the first enclosure cowslips are flowering, and there are more in the enclosure. The effect of the grazing can be seen along the path where the vegetation is shorter and many flowering plants are growing amongst the grass. An early willow warbler sings from the wood below and a startled blackbird cries as it heads for cover in the nearby overgrown orchard. Along a side path an empty shell of the heath snail is seen, with a flattish shell, coloured rings around the top side, and a wide pit in the underside. Between the two bottom stiles garlic mustard and hairy violets are flowering, but the violets in flower by the second stile are early dog-violets. Here the blackthorn is still flowering well.

The vegetation in this second enclosure is coarser and somewhat overgrown as it has yet to be grazed. As a consequence there are few plants of interest to be seen. Saplings of ash and field maple which have grown amongst the grass will be cut out soon to prevent the grassland from being shaded out. The path goes between a blackthorn thicket and a strip of hawthorn trees running down the bank on the right. This was an old hedge-line in years gone by, but due to neglect since has expanded into a thicket.

At the next stile we enter enclosure three and soon see large anthills above the path, showing up well in the shorter vegetation. There are further anthills on the grassy slopes below. A bumblebee feeds on one of the scattered dandelions. A few hairy violets seen in the dry open grassland. We pass into enclosure four where daisies are flowering in the very short turf beside the footpath.

Skylark

We continue into enclosure five. This has only recently been fenced and has yet to be grazed. The air is filled with birdsong and an early swallow skims along the hillside. After leaving the enclosure we go up to the bridleway and turn back along it. In the plum thicket there are more cowslips. By the reservoir the sweet violets have gone over. The hedge beside the bridleway was removed for a short length in years gone by and the gap now permits good views towards the north end of the Cotswolds. A kestrel hunts over the hill, and a skylark hovers over the arable field on the hill top. The bridleway turns muddy through the thicket. Where it emerges there is a pear tree in full blossom just inside enclosure two.

Tuesday 11 May

It is a hot and sunny afternoon but windy. Towards the top of the entrance slope a speckled wood butterfly guards its territory under the trees. Bulbous buttercups are flowering and cushions of wild liquorice and meadow crane's-bill will flower later in the year. The cowslips are nearly over. In enclosure one the creamy-yellow pollen on the flower spikes of glaucous sedge is noticeable. The flowerheads of the grasses are beginning to show with smooth meadow-grass predominating. The hawthorn blossom in the wood at the bottom

Wild liquorice

of the reserve comes into view. Plants flowering include herb-Robert, garlic mustard and common forget-me-not. Nearby, we hear chiffchaffs and willow warblers singing. A flock of house martins hunt for insects above the hillside.

Along the bridleway a twayblade is coming into flower. Further along, the bridleway is lined with white cow parsley and the elder bushes are starting to flower. Two peacock butterflies and a small tortoiseshell seen. Beyond the second steel gate and three metres up the trunk of a young ash are seven brown-lipped snails positioned to catch the cooling breeze. Around the foot of the gate a patch of germander speedwell makes a splash of blue. A common buckthorn is coming into flower and is attracting hoverflies, and a field maple is already flowering. A swift skims along the hillside hunting for flying insects. On the way back to the road speckled wood, small tortoiseshell and brimstone butterflies are seen.

Sunday 13 June

In enclosure one the yellow of bird's-foot-trefoil and rough hawkbit are very noticeable. Red clover flowers by the path, and the first pink spikes of pyramidal orchid are beginning to show. An occasional small heath and a number of large skipper butterflies flit around among the tall grasses with several day-flying moths.

Oxeye daisies and quaking-grass are seen, together with the first small white flowers of fairy flax

and the pale yellow ones of hop trefoil. In the enclosure a bee orchid is coming into flower and a bit further on two bee orchids grow together on the upper edge of the path, one with two flowers, and the other exceptionally early one has five flowers, some going over. Several empty chrysalid cases of burnet moths are attached to the top part of tall grass stems.

On entering the second enclosure we see a change in the vegetation. This enclosure has not been grazed for a few decades and the grass is coarse and matted; the taller grasses are false oat-grass, cock's-foot and tor-grass with some upright brome, but hardly a flower is to be seen. The old hedge-line of hawthorn and blackthorn has flowering elder and black bryony among the bushes.

Enclosure three has been grazed a number of times in the past few years and the grass is now less coarse and flowers are more plentiful. Upright brome dominates with much bird's-foot-trefoil and rough hawkbit, with white and pink spikes of common spotted-orchid by the bottom fence.

Enclosure four was grazed last autumn and the grass is short enough for abundant daisies to flower near the paths. The first field scabious flower of the year has attracted a bumblebee and a burnet moth to feed on its nectar. Bird's-foot-trefoil, upright brome and rough hawkbit are dominant with some fairy flax and quaking-grass.

Wednesday 7 July

The afternoon is overcast and not as warm is it might be for the time of

year. The wild carrots cover the bank on the left side of the track and we check to see how many have the single red floret in the centre of their flat white umbel. With them are yellow spikes of the pea-like flowers of tall melilot. Round the edges of the scrub are the biggish scrambling plants of wild liquorice with their cream pea-like flowers. This species is very scattered and local in Worcestershire but plentiful on the reserve, which is probably its best county site.

Inside the enclosure the grassland is now at its best. The predominant flower colour is yellow from rough hawkbit and bird's-foot-trefoil but there are plenty of pink spikes of pyramidal orchids and along the path red patches of clover. The number of butterflies is disappointing because

of the weather, but marbled whites are fresh, plentiful, and conspicuous with bold black markings on a white background.

Saturday 7 August

The entrance is colourful in the afternoon sunshine with common knapweed, hoary ragwort, wild carrot, bristly oxtongue and hawkweed oxtongue all in flower on one side, and traveller's-joy on the other.

Butterfly numbers are down slightly, but there is more diversity, particularly in enclosure one. Small skipper, wall brown, brown argus, common blue, meadow brown, peacock, gatekeeper, small white and large white butterflies all seen in small numbers.

The huge felted flower heads on the woolly thistles are now alive with bumblebees and butterflies feeding from the tubular purple flowers. The wall brown butterflies love to bask in the sun on the bare ground of the track and are loath to leave it. They fly up in front of us as we approach to alight a bit further along only to be disturbed once more. This continues to the end of their territory when they reluctantly circle round us to return to the track behind.

Saturday 18 September

There is a slight breeze and only hazy sunshine this afternoon. The hoary ragworts and common knapweeds up the side of the access are now going over. The tall plants of wild carrot have nearly all formed seed and closed up their umbels. It is noticeable now that autumn is beginning as the berries are starting to colour up. Along the upper part of the access can be seen the black bryony berries turning red, wild privet black, the elder black, and hips and haws red.

Saturday 9 October

This morning is dry and fairly still with sunny periods. The leaves on the trees are changing colour and starting to fall and the berries are now coloured up. The air is very clear after the rain giving good views over the Vale. On the wet ground, the snails are still out feeding with a Kentish snail and heath snails in dead heads and on plant stems. A meadow grasshopper jumps out of the way.

Enclosure five looks a bit like a battlefield as a flock of 50 sheep has recently been introduced to graze it for the first time for 30 years or so. There are no flowers left in here after their attention and the long grass already has some shorter patches.

At the bridleway we turn back. It is quite muddy because of the rain and the passage of horses. There are some strawberry clover plants which are now noticeable with their inflated pink seed-heads like little ripening strawberries.

Sunday 14 November

A clear and dry but quite windy afternoon. The down from the traveller's-joy bushes along the road and reserve entrance has been partly stripped by the wind and lies 5 cm deep in the road edge, covering big areas of the verges. Most leaves have now gone from the trees.

As we climb the stile into enclosure one we can see the extent of the floods in the riverside meadows which have taken most people by surprise. The farmers are out driving through the water to check and rescue their sheep. Half-way across the enclosure there are fine views of the hills in the distance, the Cotswolds, Bredon and the Malverns. Nearer to hand the villages of Harvington and Salford Priors just across the river are crystal clear in the clean air and low sun.

Above the windward side of the escarpment a couple of kestrels hang in the sky, occasionally losing station when the wind buffets them.

Sunday 19 December

It is a windy afternoon but dry after recent rain. A trail of fresh bedding grass leads to the badger sett past the heap of old bedding material they have dumped outside. The bramble bushes are about the only woody plants with any leaves.

In enclosure three a few dead heads of common knapweed stand up above the grass but there is little else to attract attention. One or two more hawthorn trees in the wood below have fallen down. Following the recent grazing the bare tops of the anthills stand out in enclosure five. A goldfinch is seen in the plum thicket at the south end and a blackbird flies startled out of the bushes.

Traveller's-joy seed-heads

Sunday 16 January 1994

After the recent rains the afternoon has turned out dry and fairly sunny with a slight breeze. The reserve seems now in limbo with little to see or hear. Hips remain on the roses and outside the badger set are heaps of soggy old bedding material. The air is a bit hazy in the winter sun and the distant hills cannot be seen.

In enclosure one the grass looks shorter, possibly as a result of the attention of rabbits out of the derelict orchard plus being beaten down by the rain and wind. Under the trees the new green leaves of lords-and-ladies have emerged. Our return along the bridleway is tiring as we try to find somewhere dry to walk amongst the churned up mud (and to keep the hole in my wellington boot above water!).

Robin

Thursday 24 February

It is a cloudy afternoon but dry for a change, with an easterly breeze. All the paths and tracks are slippery and muddy except for the reserve entrance which has stood up to the wet weather and horses hooves very well since it was stoned. There is evidence of the badgers making new holes at the sett and some of their tracks are now easily seen as their footsteps have made them a bit muddy. The stinking iris plant which appeared under the trees a couple of years ago has quite long leaves on it which stand out green in the dark of the scrub.

Saturday 19 March

This is more like a spring morning – dry and sunny although somewhat breezy. The traveller's-joy lining the right of entrance now has noticeable light green shoots on its old stems and the elder bushes are quite leafy. Lords-and-ladies under the bushes are full-grown and will soon be starting to flower. A wild gooseberry bush has stems well-clothed with small bright young leaves between its light-coloured spines.

In enclosure one the old grass is fairly short and beaten down by the wind but new green shoots are beginning to push through everywhere. A robin sings nearby and a wren sings in the thicket. On the hillside above the path beyond the thicket the morning sun reflected from the old grass dazzles the eye.

Just before the stile into enclosure three there is a group of freshly emerged woolly thistles with glistening water droplets on the leaf wool, and a few plants of salad burnet form green cushions with their almost full sized leaves.